The Elements of
Persuasion

The Elements of Persuasion

William A. Covino

University of Illinois at Chicago

Allyn and Bacon

Boston   London   Toronto   Sydney   Tokyo   Singapore

Vice President: Eben W. Ludlow
Marketing Manager: Lisa Kimball
Production Administrator: Annette Joseph
Editorial-Production Service: Susan Freese, Communicáto, Ltd.
Text Design and Electronic Composition: Denise Hoffman
Composition Buyer: Linda Cox
Manufacturing Buyer: Megan Cochran
Cover Administrator: Suzanne Harbison

Library of Congress Cataloging-in-Publication Data

Covino, William A.
     The elements of persuasion / William A. Covino.
         p.   cm. — (Elements of composition)
     Includes index.
     ISBN 0–205–19661–6 (alk. paper)
     1. Debates and debating. 2. Persuasion (Rhetoric). 3. Persuasion
(Psychology). I. Title. II. Series.
PN4181.C66   1997
808—dc21   97–13582
                                                                                CIP

Printed in the United States of America
10 9 8 7 6 5 4 3 2 1   02 01 00 99 98 97

Permissions Acknowledgments: **p. 8,** Maytag advertisement reprinted with the permission of
Leo Burnett Company, Inc., and Rae Lindsay. **pp. 77–87,** excerpts reprinted with permission
of Simon & Schuster from *Do the Right Thing* by Spike Lee with Lisa Jones. Copyright © 1989
by Spike Lee.

Contents

Preface

The Elements of Persuasion provides students with a concise introduction to major theories of persuasion; analyses of political, cultural, and literary events that represent the significance and scope of persuasion; and a range of questions and exercises that develop critical reading and writing skills.

Chapter 1 offers a general view of persuasion, illustrating the contributions of Aristotle's *Rhetoric,* J. L. Austin's speech act theory, and Kenneth Burke's dramatism, with current examples from political oratory, advertising, and hypothetical situations, as well as an extensive analysis of the dramatism of the O. J. Simpson criminal trial. Given this foundation, students should be able to begin an alert analysis of persuasion as it operates in public discourse and to assess the elements of persuasion in their own writing.

Subsequent chapters provide further illustration and explication of the elements of persuasion introduced in Chapter 1. The terms to which readers return throughout the book are *ethos, pathos, logos, metaphor, anaphora, kairos, illocution, perlocution, identification, scope,* and *circumference.* All are given brief definitions in the Glossary.

This book offers an analytical discussion of a representative range of persuasion events in order to feature persuasion as a wide-ranging phenomenon and to offer students principles for their own analyses. The texts discussed include the 1925 Scopes trial (Chapter 2), Jane Austen's *Persuasion* (3), Spike Lee's *Do the Right Thing* (3), the National Football League's 1996 Super Bowl (4), and the 1996 State of the Union address (5). With these texts in view, students examine the ways in which persuasion is affected by belief, desire, class, gender, and race. Austen's novel might be usefully adopted as a course reading, and video versions of Lee's film, current sports or entertainment telecasts, and current presidential addresses might be presented as opportunities to extend the discussion initiated by *The Elements of Persuasion.* Such supplemental readings and screenings are optional, however, because each of the major texts discussed is fully summarized within each chapter, and in the case of the State of the Union address, the full speech is included.

Class discussions may focus on the questions and exercises found at the end of each chapter:

- Questions to Ask Yourself invites students to (1) consider the ways in which the chapter itself employs the elements of persuasion it explains and (2) apply material from the chapter to other texts, experiences, and events.

- The Writing Exercise provides a topic related to the chapter and asks students to write a paper of 750–1,250 words.

- Persuasive Strategies for Student Writers offers suggestions and exercises that writing groups and individuals can use to analyze their own writing in progress. These may be applied to any piece of academic writing, including the Writing Exercise.

The Elements of Persuasion is an introductory work that can be assigned in a number of different college classes. Written in a style that is accessible to lower-division students yet engaging for more advanced students, this book can be assigned as the central or supplementary text in a first-year, intermediate, or advanced composition course; an introductory course in political science, psychology, or communications theory; or an introduction to rhetorical theory.

Acknowledgments

I would like to thank the following individuals, who reviewed the manuscript for Allyn and Bacon: Rolf Norgaard, University of Colorado at Boulder; Duane Roen, Arizona State University; and Irene Ward, Kansas State University.

1

Grammars of Persuasion

In one episode of *Leave It to Beaver*, the very popular 1950s sitcom now recycled in reruns, Beaver Cleaver refuses his parents' pleas to wear a suit and tie to the junior high school sports awards banquet because he and his schoolmates have agreed among themselves to look cool by not dressing up. But when he arrives at the banquet, the other boys *are* wearing suits and ties. Feeling distinctly out of place, Beaver asks his father to take him home, whereupon the wise parent—who had anticipated this situation—pulls a suit out of the trunk of the car and saves the day.

Before leaving for the banquet, Beaver had rejected what many would consider sensible arguments from his brother, mother, and father—all insisting that dressing up was appropriate for a formal occasion like this. However, simply the *sight* of his dressed-up classmates seems to persuade Beaver immediately. How does persuasion work in the situation dramatized here? Let me offer a provisional explanation to get at the nature and complexity of persuasion and to introduce some of the elements of persuasion that this book will address.

What appears to be stubbornness on Beaver's part is really a kind of logic. His behavior in this case is driven by what logicians call a *major premise*—that is, a statement that he assumes is true and that governs his conclusions about how to dress. The major premise might be expressed as "Conformity with peers is imperative." Based on his pact with his classmates, Beaver also holds onto a *minor premise* related to the specific situation: "Conformity at the banquet means wearing no suit." From these two premises, Beaver derives this conclusion: "Wearing no suit is imperative." One reason that Beaver won't listen to the reasoning offered by his family is that he and they hold no *shared premise*. Their lines of reasoning do not overlap at all.

When Beaver reaches the banquet, the scene he encounters changes his conclusion, from "Wearing *no* suit is imperative" to "Wearing a suit *is* imperative." The new reasoning at work might go like this:

Conformity with peers is imperative.

Conformity at the banquet means wearing a suit.

Wearing a suit at the banquet is imperative.

Even though no one makes a deliberate verbal argument to Beaver at the banquet, it is clear that he has changed his mind. Although his major premise remains intact, his minor premise—a situation-specific definition of *conformity*—changes, and so his conclusion changes.

This three-part structure of premises and conclusion is called a *categorical syllogism* and is the basis of *syllogistic reasoning*. Persuasion can be thought of as the process of altering the operative syllogism in a given situation, and it is clear from the *Beaver* example that persuasion can take place without anyone presenting a deliberate argument. So, for instance, if the weather report on my car radio announces the strong possibility of heavy rain just as I am leaving home for the day, I might be persuaded to step back inside and take an umbrella. Perhaps this behavior might also be explained syllogistically, with premises and conclusion, as follows:

Staying dry is comfortable.

An umbrella will help me stay dry.

An umbrella will help me stay comfortable.

But this syllogism leaves out a number of other considerations that might figure into the persuasive effect of the weather report: Perhaps I think the rain might ruin the appearance of my hair and clothes; perhaps I think others will view me as strange if I let myself get wet; perhaps the umbrella was a gift from a friend, and I'd like to show it off in her presence as an indication of gratitude; perhaps the umbrella isn't for me but for my child, whom I fear will be walking home from school without one; perhaps I'm following an old family superstition that wet hair causes pneumonia; perhaps I've just read a magazine article about acid rain and imagine searing droplets burning through my clothes. Perhaps to maintain a natty appearance I *always* carry an umbrella, and the weather report reminded me to bring it. Perhaps a combination of some of these possibilities affects my action. In any case, it is clear that *an instance of persuasion can involve the complex interaction of premises, intentions, beliefs, assumptions, and experiences.*

Understanding the elements of persuasion may be more crucial for us in the nineties than ever. This is because today we are well beyond the simple views of values and decisions represented by *Beaver;* we now see ourselves living in a *quantum* universe, whose physical properties and processes are not fixed and predictable but complex and changeable. To the extent that we see our world as a complex of *contingencies*—that is, events that are partly determined by the different human psychologies involved: by chance, by accident, by the influence of unknown or uncertain forces—we regard any decision we make as not simply good or bad, true or false, right or wrong but as more complex than any either/or set of terms allows. Because no particular outcome can be absolute or guaranteed, we often find that we must gamble on the *probability* that a matter will go one way or another. What if the weather report announces only a 40 percent chance of rain? Should I grab my umbrella? Or what if Beaver Cleaver had found that some of his classmates were dressed up but others weren't? Would it have mattered how many and which ones were dressed up? On a more serious level, consider U.S. policies on war-torn regions such as Bosnia, which was formerly Yugoslavia. Such policies are reconsidered almost daily because the conditions and balances of power affecting tensions there are always changing. There are no clear good guys or bad guys, no clear sense of whether a given country should take moral and economic responsibility for the hardships of the region and, if so, how and to what extent. In such complex situations, what distinguishes a more persuasive argument from a less persuasive one?

One of the most important factors determining the effectiveness of persuasion is the identity of the *agent*. Who or what is trying to change my mind? is a question that operates consciously or unconsciously in every instance of persuasion. Sometimes, we seem to assign persuasive intent to nonhuman forces. If I say "The weather report persuaded me to carry an umbrella," I am suggesting that there is a purposeful intention motivating the report. This could be the case if we imagine that the radio broadcaster delivering the report sees helping people make choices about weather gear as part of her job. But there are numerous times when we accord purposeful intention, or agency, to a completely unintelligent source, as when we say things like "The snow persuaded me to stay inside" or "The chocolate bon-bons in the center of the table persuaded me to have some dessert" or, in a case like Beaver Cleaver's, "All those suits persuaded me to change clothes." Such statements stress our tendency to think of persuasion as something done to us, rather than something we do to ourselves by, for instance, maintaining and constructing syllogisms that enforce certain conclusions.

This book will maintain that persuasion is a process that we do to ourselves—that whenever you are the *object* of persuasion, you are also the *agent*. With this position, I am not proposing that anyone who is persuaded to act mistakenly or immorally should carry all the blame for that action. However, I do mean to emphasize that a critical understanding of the elements of persuasion can help us step back and analyze our own susceptibility as well as our own role in changing the minds of others.

The history of persuasion coincides with the history of *rhetoric* because from its origins in Greek antiquity, rhetoric was understood as the art of persuasion. In about 350 BCE, the Greek philosopher Aristotle offered a distinction between *rhetoric* and *persuasion* that will serve us here. He said that the function of rhetoric "is not to persuade but to see the available means of persuasion." He understood that rhetoric is often confused with the act of persuasion but insisted instead that the rhetorician's job is to discover what sorts of statements and conditions could be conducive to persuasion in any given case. This rather subtle distinction between rhetoric and persuasion may indicate Aristotle's recognition that persuasion itself is a very uncertain process, one that cannot be guaranteed. That is, learning rhetoric does not ensure that we will become more persuasive because every specific persuasion situation is full of contingencies that cannot be accounted for in advance. Yet as we will see in a more extensive look at Aristotle in the next section, certain psychological considerations are generally applicable in a wide variety of situations.

One of the reasons that persuasion is possible on a mass scale—that a number of different people may be persuaded to make the same decision—is that we tend to share a stock of *premises* that can lead us to similar conclusions. As the modern philosopher and rhetorician Kenneth Burke says in his book *Counter-Statement,* "Generally the ideology of an individual is a slight variant of the ideology distinguishing the class among which he arose" (1968, p. 162). Drawing from both Burke and Aristotle, we might say that any individual's beliefs, values, desires, and expectations—what Aristotle associates with *pathos* and Burke with *ideology*—influence his or her susceptibility to persuasion. Any group of individuals that shares what Burke calls common *patterns of experience* (which include social status, education, and cultural background) is likely to share common susceptibilities to persuasion. The members of such a group will tend to reach similar conclusions and make similar decisions in a number of cases. We are all members of more than one group; for instance, we all belong to groups as large as the human race and as small as our own households. With the understanding that we are all members of different groups with differing patterns of experience, Aristotle attempted what was perhaps the first broad analysis of mass ideology: to propose what kinds of general elements are at work in the process of persuasion.

Aristotle's *Rhetoric*

As Aristotle makes clear in his *Rhetoric,* persuasion is necessary whenever auditors (listeners, readers, viewers) are faced with a *choice.* This may be a choice involving a particular action; that is, I might be persuaded to vote for a certain candidate, to mow the lawn today rather than tomorrow, or to order chicken rather than fish. Or the choice may involve preferring one interpretation of a situation over others, without necessarily taking direct action in response. For example, upon viewing Frank Capra's film *It's a Wonderful Life,* I may be persuaded that it's a celebration of one man's egotism, rather than a heartwarming tribute to hope and love. Or upon reading Mary Shelley's *Frankenstein*, I may be persuaded that the monster is a sympathetic representative of human loneliness, rather than a symbol of the destructive male ego or a hideous warning against the excesses of science.

Aristotle understands that all persuasion involves interpretive constructions of presented material and that the same presentation can lead to different kinds of conclusions from different audiences. He concentrates on situations in which one person tries to persuade others through delivering a formal speech and proposes that in such situations, the power of persuasion relies on the interaction of *ethos* (the character of the speaker), *pathos* (the emotions and state of mind of the audience), and *logos* (the content of the speech).

The types of speeches that Aristotle discusses are the *deliberative,* the *judicial,* and the *epideictic:*

- A *deliberative* speech focuses on decisions concerning the future and is typically delivered to a legislative body. For example, the State of the Union address delivered annually by the U.S. president is in large part deliberative, calling upon Congress to enact policies that affect the future course of the nation.

- A *judicial* speech focuses on decisions about what happened in the past and is typically delivered in a court of law. The opening and closing addresses given by attorneys in the highly publicized trials of O. J. Simpson tried to persuade the juries that Simpson either did or did not commit murder.

- An *epideictic* speech often has either praise or blame as its purpose and may differ from the other two kinds as being mainly ceremonial (for instance, a funeral oration or a holiday toast) and not exhorting any direct action (like a vote or a verdict) from the audience.

In an Aristotelian framework, a speech is never persuasive *in itself;* the very same words in the hands of different speakers or addressed to different audiences will have entirely different effects. To begin a further analysis of the interaction of *ethos, pathos,* and *logos,* let's consider this excerpt from a speech by President Ronald Reagan, addressed to the

AFL-CIO in March 1981. It is both epideictic and deliberative, a tribute to the audience and a request that they assure the future of the United States by lending their support to the current administration:

> I'm here today because I salute what you've done for America. In your work, you build. In your personal lives, you sustain the core of family and neighborhood. In your faith, you sustain our religious principles. And with your strong patriotism, you're the bulwark which supports an America second to none in the world. I believe the American people are with us in our cause. I'm confident in our ability to work together, to meet and surmount our problems, and to accomplish the goals that we all seek.
>
> Now, I know that we can't make things right overnight. But we will make them right. Our destiny is not our fate. It is our choice. And I'm asking you as I ask all Americans, in these months of decision, please join me as we take this new path. You and your forbearers built this Nation. Now, please help us rebuild it, and together we'll make America great again.

Ethos

For Aristotle, the *ethos* of a speaker is persuasive when the speech demonstrates (1) *phronesis,* or what we might call practical wisdom or common sense; (2) *arete,* or moral virtue; and (3) *eunoia,* or goodwill toward the audience. Reagan exhibits *phronesis* when he says that "we can't make things right overnight," acknowledging that he's not so fool-hardy as to believe that big problems have quick and easy solutions. His *arete* is evident in his identification with traditional American ideals: family, religion, patriotism. And his *eunoia* is indicated both by his compliments to the audience about their values and by his expressed willingness to work cooperatively with them: "I'm confident in our ability to work together."

Although Aristotle locates *ethos* in the words of the speech, rather than in the reputation or social position of the speaker, others have noted that these features can contribute to effective persuasion. Setting aside whether members of the audience share Reagan's conservative political philosophy, we can nonetheless say that his speech on the problems facing the United States gains considerable persuasive force simply by virtue of his office and the authority and experience identified with it.

Consider the *ethos* of this advertisement by Maytag:

After years of hard work, it's curtains for Mrs. Lindsay's Maytag washer.

Over the years, Mrs. Rae Lindsay of Englewood Cliffs, New Jersey has certainly put her Maytag washer to the test. First it was thousands and thousands of diapers. Then it was loads of baseball, soccer, track and basketball uniforms. Not to mention all the ordinary clothes that just get dirty as three kids grow up. Let's face it, after all those years of abuse it would come as no surprise if her machine was all washed up. But it's not. In fact, Mrs. Lindsay has recently challenged it with quilts, throw rugs and even curtains. And everything comes out as clean as those diapers did years ago. While we can't promise every Maytag washer will last as long as Mrs. Lindsay's, we build them all to last longer than any other brand. So if you're looking for heavy-duty performance, take Mrs. Lindsay's advice and make your next washer a Maytag. Because even after years of use, the only thing she's hanging up is those clean curtains.

MAYTAG. The Dependability People.

The *ethos* of *phronesis* is maintained throughout the text of this ad by the repeated emphasis on dependability, such that the practical wisdom of the Maytag company is supported and verified by the *ethos* of Mrs. Lindsay; "take Mrs. Lindsay's advice," we are told. Her practical wisdom is located in years of experience washing the dirty clothes of three children. The advertisement works as an epideictic speech, a kind of tribute to Mrs. Lindsay that aggrandizes her household accomplishments and the Maytag machine that assists her.

Pathos

In Greek, *pathe* means "emotions," and for Aristotle, *pathos* is an appeal to those states of mind that have an emotional component. Some of the states of mind Aristotle discusses are anger, calmness, friendliness, enmity, hate, fear, confidence, shame, shamelessness, kindliness, unkindliness, pity, indignation, envy, and emulation. With reference to current issues, we can say that a speaker warning against tax increases may want the audience to feel anger or indignation about such an expense; a sales representative for a burglar alarm company may want to arouse some measure of fear in a potential customer; and an advertisement soliciting donations for children in poverty may appeal to pity. In the case of Ronald Reagan, a political leader seeking the support of a constituency, his speech appeals to their national sense of confidence in their common values and promising future; and in the case of Mrs. Lindsay and Maytag, the emotional appeal is to emulation, which for Aristotle corresponds with the desire to have something that another similar person possesses. We seek to emulate those who are of the same sort as ourselves and for whom we have a positive regard. Maytag's Mrs. Lindsay, then, is presented in order to provoke the emulation of homemakers.

Characteristics such as age and social status are also significant features of *pathos*. People who are elderly tend to have different emotional responses than those who are young. Aristotle's description of elderly people reflects a rather grim view of life, one decidedly unflattering to them: "Having lived many years and having been more often deceived and having made more mistakes themselves and since most things turn out badly," people who are elderly tend to be cynical, suspicious, emotionally uncommitted, small minded, and hopeless. Young people, on the other hand, are impulsive, trusting, hopeful, excessive, and idealistic. Aristotle goes on to say that the wealthy tend to be arrogant, the powerful dignified, the fortunate religious (when they see the gods as the source of their good fortune).

While Aristotle's particular assessments of these types of people may be peculiar to the culture and time in which he wrote and thus questionable or even objectionable, his general point remains significant: A person's age and social status can help determine the kinds of persuasion that will be most effective for him or her. Such considerations are today routine for persons in the business of making public appeals; politicians and advertisers, for example, rely on sophisticated demographic data about their audiences and try to match the emotional nature of their appeals to the sorts of people addressed. Reagan's speech seems directed to those Aristotle would place in the "prime of life" (between about 35 and 50), who are neither recklessly impulsive nor hopelessly cynical; as Aristotle says, "They combine prudence with courage." Maytag's Mrs. Lindsay also represents the prime of life, as she is the mother of three children who last washed their diapers "years ago."

Logos

Ethos and *pathos* are both materialized in the *logos*, or what we may call the text, of the speech. The basic textual unit of persuasion is the *enthymeme*, which can be translated as "a piece of reasoning." An *enthymeme* is a kind of claim, which initiates a transaction between the speaker and the audience. The audience fills in unspoken assumptions that will verify the speaker's claim and make it acceptable—or so the speaker hopes. For instance, if Reagan's speech is to be persuasive, all of the so-called virtues he surveys—family and neighborhood, religious faith, patriotism—must be assumed to be good by the audience. In an enthymemic transaction, then, when he says "In your personal lives, you sustain the core of family and neighborhood," the audience *must* assume that their commitment to these values is worthwhile and important; otherwise, they will not be persuaded to the practical wisdom of the speaker nor will they share his apparent confidence in the future. In other words, this piece of Reagan's speech relies on a corresponding piece of belief that the audience supplies, and to the extent that they supply that missing piece, they are participating in and enacting their own persuasion.

An enthymeme can be thought of as a truncated syllogism. Remember that a syllogism is conventionally regarded as a three-part structure, with a major premise, a minor premise, and a conclusion, as in the following:

One cannot be both free and a slave.

All people are the slaves of either money or chance.

Therefore, there is no person who is free.

Delivered as an enthymeme, this set of statements could leave the major premise—"One cannot be both free and a slave"—to be supplied by the audience. Or perhaps a speaker might shorten the expression further, leaving both premises implicit and unspoken:

None of us is truly free.

This sort of one-liner is called a *maxim* by Aristotle and relies even more fully than the enthymeme on the audience's filling in the missing pieces.

An enthymeme will often exhibit an if/then structure to connect a premise to a conclusion or do so by use of prepositions such as *for, because,* and *since.* However, the enthymeme need not be explicitly framed by these terms; rather, the causal relationship of the premises to the conclusion is most effective as a psychological construction supplied by the audience, rather than a grammatical one supplied by the speaker. For Reagan's speech, his desired audience might psychologically reconstruct from the spoken words enthymemes like those that follow; doing so would indicate a participatory and agreeable understanding:

Because of your values, "you're the bulwark which supports an America second to none in the world."

Since the American people are with us in our cause, "I'm confident in our ability to work together."

"Our destiny is not our fate," *for* "it is our choice."

If you cooperate with "the goals that we all seek," *then* "we'll make America great again."

Another persuasive device that is no less effective but different in function is the *paradigm,* or, as it is more commonly known today, the *example.* For Aristotle, the effectiveness of the example rests on the audience's belief that history repeats itself. By stating historical precedents, the speaker tries to get the audience to believe that what happened before will happen again. The Maytag ad presents us with an extended example—a narrative of Mrs. Lindsay's years of washing—in order to suggest that the history of dependability can repeat itself.

Clearly, the *logos* of the speech must enact the *shared* beliefs and values of the speaker and audience. The Maytag ad, which appeared in

People—a magazine directed toward prime-of-life readers—would not likely sell many washers if it appeared in *Seventeen* or *Scientific American*. And Reagan may not have been persuasive if he had delivered his praise of family and neighborhood at a center for women who have been battered, where those concepts could have painful associations for audience members. As the modern theorist of rhetoric Chaim Perelman notes in *The Realm of Rhetoric,* "To achieve any degree of success with their audiences, arguments have to proceed from premises that are *acceptable* to their audiences" (1982, p. x). So in a sense, since an act of persuasion depends so much on the *prior* circumstances and experiences of the given members of an audience, its effectiveness or ineffectiveness has already been set up long before a speaker or writer begins to construct an argument.

Saying Makes It So?
Speech Acts and Persuasion

What is it that persuades us that an utterance is true? According to one influential theory, developed by language philosopher J. L. Austin in the 1950s, we judge an utterance to be true when it fits the situation, or context, in which it is delivered. In *How to Do Things with Words,* Austin says:

> It is essential to realize that "true" and "false," like "free" and "unfree," do not stand for anything simple at all; but only for a general dimension of being a right or proper thing to say as opposed to a wrong thing, in these circumstances, to this audience, for these purposes and with these intentions. (1962, p. 145)

For instance, imagine that the same weather forecaster who predicted rain in our earlier example also said, "Today the temperatures will stay cold." What does *cold* mean here? If it's Chicago in July, *cold* could mean temperatures in the fifties; if it's November, temperatures in the twenties would be *cold* and temperatures in the fifties would be *mild*. We can only determine the range of meanings for the word *cold* by knowing the *context* in which it is uttered.

And for Austin, the purpose and intention of an utterance are equally crucial; he continues, "The truth or falsity of a statement depends not merely on the meanings of words but on what act you were performing in what circumstances" (p. 145). That is, we tend to judge the truth or falsehood of a statement with reference to what the speaker or writer seems to be intending to *do* by saying it. Imagine a group of college students preparing to head out the door to watch the homecoming football game at the college stadium. Student X, who is just beginning to recover from the flu and would rather stay home, opens the door, shivers, and says, "It's raining outside." Student Y, who waited in line for hours to get these football tickets and doesn't want to see his efforts go to waste, says, "You call that rain? It's just a little drizzle—perfect football weather!" Student Z says, "The weather report I heard on the radio didn't mention rain," to which X answers, "The Weather Channel did." Which of the students is telling the truth?

In such a situation, each statement—even the one that seems most factual—is uttered in order *to perform* some action or actions. According to Austin's *speech act theory,* as it has come to be known, we will get a fuller picture by asking *What action is the speaker or writer attempting to perform?* rather than *Is the statement true or correct?* That is, what is true in any given situation depends on the psychological preferences, preoccupations, and needs of the persons acting within that situation. For instance, in the above exchange, Student X might be trying to perform a *request,* Y a *refusal,* and Z a *refutation.* Or might we say that X is trying to *complain,* Y to *insist,* and Z to *confirm?*

Austin gives the name *performative* to any utterance that—by virtue of being delivered—performs an action. He eventually comes to understand *all* utterances as performatives but explains that some kinds of performatives are more obvious and effective than others. When an umpire says "You're out" or a judge says "I find you guilty as charged" or a justice of the peace says "I now pronounce you husband and wife," the *saying* itself *makes it so.* But if (as is quite common) a spectator at a baseball game yells "You're out" from the stands, the utterance has no actual effect on the game. This is because certain performatives are only effective if uttered by *authorized* people. When an umpire yells "You're out," the game's players behave as if they have been persuaded that this is true because according to the rules of the game, what the umpire says counts. In other words, the extent to which we are persuaded by a given utterance can depend on the *institution*—in this case, the game of baseball—within which the utterance occurs. A judge who pronounces sentence during a trial at which she presides is acting according to the instituted rules of law, and in that context, what she says counts. In the encounter among Students X, Y, and Z, no one seems more authorized than the others to pronounce on the weather, though Y tries to give his utterance institutional authority by referring to the radio and X does so by citing the Weather Channel.

It is also true that for a performative to be effective, it must be uttered correctly, completely, and sincerely. For example, the umpire usually accompanies his call with the clenched-fist gesture that is conventional for signaling an out and means what he says. Likewise, the judge delivers a verdict from the bench seriously and in a regular, formal pattern that is conventional in her particular jurisdiction (for instance, "John Q. Public, on the count of armed robbery, this court finds you guilty as charged.").

Many of us regularly utter performatives outside the formal institutional circumstances that govern the umpire and the judge (for instance, when we make promises). And it is always true that for the performative to count, it must be uttered conventionally, completely, correctly, and sincerely by an appropriate person. The question that occupies us here is: If all of these conditions are operating, does that mean that the utterance is necessarily persuasive?

Addressing this question will require a fuller survey of the kinds of performatives in regular use. One of the most common is the *promise*. If I say, in all sincerity, "I promise to arrive by 5 P.M.," the *saying* of the promise is the *performing* of the promise. Performing the promise is not the same as actually arriving by 5 P.M., but regardless of whether the promised action does or does not take place, the utterance counts as a promise.

This sort of utterance is an *explicit* performative because the performative phrase itself—*I promise*—is part of the utterance. Here are some other explicit performatives:

I'm warning you to clean up that room right now.

I'm giving you one more chance.

I order you to fire.

I hereby declare this National Education Week.

I hereby christen this ship the *USS Republic*.

I give up.

I apologize.

When Ronald Reagan says to the AFL-CIO, "I salute what you've done for America" and "I'm asking you as I ask all Americans," he is performing the acts of saluting and asking. In most cases, however, the *performative force* of an utterance is *implicit* rather than *explicit*. When a military commander says "Fire!" during a battle, he is generally understood to be performing an order. But the force of a performative is not always unambiguous. "Clean up your room," uttered in a serious tone by a parent to a child, may be either an order or a warning, or perhaps both.

Often, a speech act is not only implicit but *indirect*, as well. The explicit command "I'm ordering you to turn down the stereo" becomes implicit when expressed as "Turn down the stereo" and might be expressed indirectly in any of the following ways:

The stereo is pretty loud.

Would you mind turning down the stereo?

I can't hear myself think.

Does the stereo have to be that loud?

It sure is noisy in here.

It's hard to enjoy the music when it's that loud.

Speech acts become most interesting as vehicles for persuasion when we consider how difficult it is to pin down what act an utterance is actually performing in a given situation. Imagine a student arriving a few minutes late for class, after the professor has already begun the day's discussion. As the student enters the room, the professor stops, smiles at the student, and says, "Welcome." What act is being performed here? Presuming that the professor is sincere (which may well be true), this is an act of greeting. However, later on, the late student speaks to a classmate and says, "The professor really embarrassed me today," whereupon the classmate says, "Yeah, I guess he really convinced you to arrive on time from now on."

What happens here points to the difference between two kinds of *locutions,* what Austin calls the *illocutionary act* and the *perlocutionary act. Illocution* refers to the *conventional force* of an utterance, that is, its apparent function—in this case, a greeting. *Perlocution* is a much more unwieldy phenomenon, referring to the effect of the utterance on a listener or reader. In this case, the teacher's greeting affected the student as an act of embarrassment and her classmate as an act of convincing. The point is that a given utterance can be understood to perform a number of different acts simultaneously.

With illocution and perlocution in mind, we can compare the apparent force of an utterance with its actual force. This becomes necessary when we consider how much of our speaking is the performance of indirect speech acts. As linguist Deborah Tannen points out in *That's Not What I Meant* (1986), most of the time we don't say what we mean, for a number of reasons:

1. Being indirect avoids confrontation. Saying, for instance, "I'm not sure I'll be available to help" is less likely to start a fight than "I refuse."

2. Being direct can be insensitive to others' feelings.

3. It's impractical and perhaps impossible to convey meaning fully and directly because so much is behind every statement we make.

This becomes evident in the typical exchange that most parents have experienced with their young children:

Parent: Go wash your hands.

Child: Why?

Parent: Because they need to be clean for dinner.

Child: Why?

Parent: Because you shouldn't get dirt on your food.

Child: Why?

Usually, an exchange like this ends with "Because I said so," the parent exasperated with the impossibility of giving a full, direct account. Similarly, in the earlier example, Student X does not say "I'm asking that we stay home from the football game," which might require a laboriously extended explanation and perhaps a confrontation, but instead issues the request indirectly by noticing inclement weather.

British novelist Jane Austen, who wrote during the early nineteenth century, was particularly sensitive to how rarely the apparent force of an utterance is the same as its actual force. She writes about relationships between men and women who are trying to figure out one another and who are constantly drawing mistaken conclusions. For Austen, misunderstanding is a fact of human communication and is often illustrated as a mismatch between what I have been calling *illocution* and *perlocution*. In Volume 2, Chapter 10 of *Persuasion* (1818), a novel that we will examine more extensively later in this book, Mary Musgrove insists to her husband Charles that he had promised to accompany her to a social gathering; Charles responds, "No, I did not promise. I only smirked and bowed, and said the word 'happy.' There was no promise." Here, Mary Musgrove claims to have understood her husband's various gestures and mutterings as the performance of a promise, while he responds that his words and actions did not add up to a promise at all. With the title of this novel, Austen is suggesting that persuasion is a central problem in social conversation and inviting us to ask questions about what accounts for effective, ineffective, or misunderstood persuasion among her characters.

To mention a literary artist here as a guide to the elements of persuasion may seem unusual, since many regard literature as fiction rather than real life, in which persuasion that is connected to real-world events can take place. However, it is important to realize, as literary theorist Stanley Fish has argued, that in real life we each carry with us a kind of story—that is, a set of experiences, conclusions, values, interpretations, and rules that constitute the way we perceive and evaluate and that determine our own actions, or *performances*. As Shakespeare declared in the famous lines "All the world's a stage, And all the men and women merely players" and as modern philosopher and critic Kenneth Burke proposed in this century, we are all characters in a drama, persuading and interpreting, using the partial knowledge that is at our disposal.

Kenneth Burke's Dramatism

Writing during the middle of this century, Kenneth Burke was concerned with *symbolic action,* which is any action we perform, express, or understand through words. In his writing, he stresses that any instance of symbolic action is full of ambiguity; that is, any use of language can be interpreted in a number of different ways. When any of us is persuaded, it is because we have interpreted a spoken or written action in a particular way, which we have chosen from among a number of possibilities. Understanding an action in a particular way means giving it a specific name. For instance, when the price of IBM stock fell during 1992 and 1993, some investors called the price change a *disaster,* while others called it an *opportunity.* Burke would say that these different names represent different *dramas* that investors constructed to interpret the fall in price. As he explains in *A Grammar of Motives* (1969, p. xv), each drama consists of the interrelation of five elements, or categories:

Act:	"What took place, in thought or deed"
Scene:	"The background of the act, the situation in which it occurred"
Agent:	"What person or kind of person performed the act"
Agency:	"What means or instruments [were] used"
Purpose:	"What motivated the act"

Burke realizes that there is no one way to fill in any of these categories:

> [People] may violently disagree about the purposes behind a given act, or about the character of the person who did it, or how he did it, or in what situation he acted; or they may even insist upon totally different words to name the act itself. (p. xv)

Consider first the kind of investor who might respond negatively to a drop in the price of IBM: He holds substantial shares of IBM stock and fears that the downward movement signals continuing reduced confidence in the company, brought on by successful competition by younger companies for the technology market. He responds to the price drop as a warning that he should invest elsewhere and sells his IBM shares. The second investor may be the sort who holds no IBM stock but is thinking of investing in a high-profile technology company. She has been examining a twenty-year chart of price fluctuations for IBM and concludes that IBM has consistently responded well to challenges from competitors and is likely to rise significantly in future years. Concluding that buying at this historic low will mean significant future profits, she invests in IBM.

Using Burke's pentad, we can say that the first investor understands the Act as a disastrous drop in the price of IBM stock. The Scene that motivates (as Burke would say) this naming of the Act is, in a larger sense, the competitive technology market, and, in a more specific sense, the financial stake that the investor has in IBM. Both of these are backgrounds that motivate his particular naming of the Act. The Agent here is understood as a collective, rather than an individual person, that is, as investors lacking confidence in IBM. The Agency, or means for communicating this drop in price, is the New York Stock Exchange. The Purpose—for this investor—is to warn investors away from IBM. Represented schematically, the pentad looks like this:

Act: Disastrous drop in the price of IBM stock

Scene: (1) A competitive technology market
        (2) Substantial investment capital in IBM

Agent: Discouraged IBM investors

Agency: New York Stock Exchange

Purpose: Warning against IBM investment

By contrast, Investor 2 understands the change in the IBM price as an opportune drop. The Scene that motivates this naming of the act is, as in the case of the first investor, twofold: (1) the long-term price history of IBM and (2) the availability of investment capital. The Agent may be the same here—investors lacking confidence in IBM—but the difference is that Investor 2 does not share that lack of confidence. The Agency is, once again, the New York Stock Exchange. But the Purpose—in Investor 2's mind—is to invite investment in IBM. Investor 2's pentad looks like this:

Act: An opportune drop in the price of IBM stock

Scene: (1) The history of IBM prices
        (2) Available money to invest

Agent: (Mistakenly) discouraged IBM investors

Agency: New York Stock Exchange

Purpose: Inviting investment in IBM

Imagine Investor 1 shouting "Sell, sell, sell" and Investor 2 shouting "Buy, buy, buy," and you have a picture of the same phenomenon persuading different people to draw entirely contradictory conclusions.

Dramatistic Constructions of the O. J. Simpson Criminal Trial

A well-publicized recent event—the verdict in the O. J. Simpson criminal trial—has been named in a number of different ways, reflecting the effects of different persuasive dramas constructed by people who followed the trial. Simpson, football hero and show business celebrity, was tried for the June 1994 murder of his ex-wife, Nicole Brown Simpson, and an acquaintance of hers, Ronald Goldman. The trial began in September 1994 and concluded in September 1995. The prosecution argued that Simpson's history of spousal abuse, the blood evidence found at Simpson's property, and the absence of an alibi for Simpson's whereabouts during the crime all pointed clearly to guilt. The defense argued that sloppy evidence collection by the Los Angeles Police Department (LAPD), a history of racism attached to one of the chief investigators, and a number of gaps in the prosecution's case all indicated a reasonable doubt that Simpson had committed the crime, which should compel the jury to acquit him.

The trial lasted for just over a year and sometimes involved the presentation of highly technical evidence. Members of the jury repeatedly voiced their dismay to Judge Lance Ito over the length of the trial, and several were dismissed and replaced by alternates before the case was concluded. After the case was submitted to them, the jury engaged in formal deliberations for just under four hours before returning a verdict of not guilty.

The entire trial was telecast on cable television; millions of viewers tuned in daily, and there was continuous public discussion and speculation over Simpson's guilt or innocence. Viewers who kept up with the evidence considered themselves to be as well informed as the jury (perhaps *too* well informed from a strict legal standpoint, given that viewers were able to witness courtroom proceedings and out-of-court commentary that was kept from the jury, that is, information that was legally inadmissible). Announcement of the verdict was telecast by all the major television networks and carried widely on radio. Never before had the process of judicial persuasion been featured so prominently as a national spectacle.

The verdict of not guilty—announced by the clerk of the court and then verified by a poll of each individual on the jury—created a national response. As expected, many people disagreed strongly with the verdict, while many others found it appropriate. Emotions on both sides were strong.

Those inside the courtroom who had been consistent supporters of Simpson—his family and friends—were very happy with the verdict, while the family and friends of the victims were deeply distressed. We tend not to regard these people's responses as consequences of persuasion because they are not impartial observers, like the jury is presumed to be. But the larger viewing audience clearly saw themselves, rightly or wrongly, as a kind of national jury whose opinions about Simpson's guilt or innocence were shaped by the evidence and arguments of the trial. During the days following the verdict, debates and discussions about it could be heard all over the United States, on television and radio as well as in homes, stores, and offices. And for the most part, these discussions concerned how to *name* what had taken place. Here are some posttrial comments overheard in various public places:

> That verdict wasn't about justice, it was about what money can buy.

> This is a victory for every black person who's ever been discriminated against.

> The verdict is proof that tabloid television can't convict a man of what he didn't do.

> I can only call that verdict a poor excuse for justice.

> That verdict was a slap in the face of the LAPD.

Comments like these indicate that different people were somehow persuaded to name the verdict in very different ways. We can survey the elements of persuasion that may lead to one way of naming the Simpson verdict rather than another by using Burke's pentad to construct different sets of dramatistic relationships, or *ratios.*

To begin with, here is a pentad that attempts a *neutral* or *objective* naming of Act, Agent, Scene, Agency, and Purpose:

Pentad 1

Act:	Not-guilty verdict
Agent:	The jury
Scene:	Los Angeles Superior Court
Agency:	Reading of the verdict by the clerk of the court
Purpose:	Acquitting O. J. Simpson of criminal charges

However, most people involved in the trial would not give such neutral assessments of these categories. For instance, some regarded the Purpose of the verdict as correcting for the historically unfair treatment that blacks have received in the U.S. legal system. If we call this the Purpose, the other labels change, too. For instance, the Act is understood no longer as the flat delivery of a verdict but as a mode of speaking out for equal treatment under the law. The Agent, Agency, and Scene are different, as well:

Pentad 2

Purpose:	Correcting for the historically unfair treatment of blacks
Act:	Speaking out for equal treatment under the law
Agent:	Representatives of revolutionary racial justice
Agency:	The criminal court system
Scene:	The racist United States

Someone who wanted to write an argument based on this drama of relations between members of the pentad might say:

The O. J. Simpson verdict served to foster national recognition of the historically unfair treatment of blacks in the racist United States. The jury, guided by the rules of criminal justice, became representatives of *racial* justice, as well. Speaking through the authority of the criminal court system, their verdict carried the weight of law while it issued a revolutionary message: fair and equal treatment for all citizens.

Imagine someone reading this statement and responding, "That jury wasn't after racial justice, they were just tired." (In fact, a number of media commentators have speculated on the effect of the jury's fatigue on the verdict.) Changing the name of the Agent affects the other members of the pentad and creates yet another drama of relationships:

Pentad 3

Agent:	A severely fatigued jury
Purpose:	To end the trial and return home as soon as possible
Act:	A verdict that does not reflect careful re-examination of the evidence
Agency:	Deliberations lasting four hours or less
Scene:	The longest sequestration in United States legal history

Now imagine someone who has a slightly different take on the persuasive drama at work here; he says, "That jury wasn't tired, they were angry! The prosecution just took too long." His renaming of the agent implies another pentad:

Pentad 4

Agent:	An angry jury
Act:	Emotion overcoming reason
Agency:	Quick deliberation
Scene:	A protracted prosecution case
Purpose:	To refuse the prosecution's appeal to examine the evidence

One of the overheard comments mentioned earlier targets the LAPD, suggesting that the verdict was a response to the sloppy police investigative and forensics work that the defense team alleged. That view generates this pentad:

Pentad 5

Act:	Condemning the Los Angeles Police Department
Agent:	The Simpson defense team
Agency:	A not-guilty verdict (Note that what was the Act in other pentads becomes the Agency here.)
Scene:	LAPD investigative team and forensics lab
Purpose:	Acquittal of O. J. Simpson

And then there was the person who emphasized that the Simpson verdict illustrates "what money can buy," thus implying this pentad:

Pentad 6

Agency:	Several hundred thousand dollars
Act:	Retaining a high-priced defense team
Agent:	O. J. Simpson
Scene:	The market for legal representation
Purpose:	Acquittal

Frequently during the trial, coverage was called a "media circus." This view gives us a label for the Scene that generates a pentad emphasizing the role of the media in the verdict:

Pentad 7

Scene:	A media circus
Act:	Featuring the Simpson verdict as crucial national news
Agency:	Live television and radio broadcasts
Agent:	Television and radio networks
Purpose:	Raising viewer and listener ratings

In closing arguments, the prosecution emphasized a pattern of spousal abuse against Nicole Brown Simpson by O. J. Simpson, replaying a phone call that Nicole had made to the 9-1-1 emergency number and showing photographs of Nicole in which she was horribly bruised. With this evidence, the prosecution tried to define the act of murder as the predictable outcome of a history of abuse and to suggest to the jury that the verdict must recognize and condemn such abuse. The not-guilty verdict was regarded by many, especially women's rights groups, as a rejection of the importance and relevance of spousal abuse. One juror emphatically declared after the trial that spousal abuse was an irrelevant issue, indicating that she and others had *rejected* the definition of the Act of murder represented in the following pentad:

Pentad 8

Act:	The ultimate outcome of spousal abuse
Scene:	History of Nicole's abuse by O. J. Simpson
Agent:	O. J. Simpson
Agency:	Murder
Purpose:	Maintaining power over one's spouse

Burke admits that his pentad is aimed at complexity, not clarity. His own key terms—Act, Scene, Agent, Agency, and Purpose—are shifty; none can be defined absolutely. Taking *war* as an example, Burke notes that when we think of war as "a means to an end," it is an Agency; as a particular or collective action, it is an Act; as the goal of an aggressive government, it is a Purpose; for someone inducted into the army during wartime, it is a Scene; and when it is represented in certain mythologies as a god or goddess, war is an Agent. As for the categories of the pentad, it is true that Agent is most obviously understood as a person or persons but might also be understood, for instance, as an abstract emotion or ideal that motivates some Act. So the Agent of an Act of censorship might be understood as "fear," while the Agent of a poem might be called "imagination." When generating pentads, the point is to multiply ways of naming, not restrict them.

The Burkean pentad allows us to speculate about how others can be persuaded by surveying the various dramas that certain kinds of people in certain circumstances might construct. But more importantly, the pentad allows us to understand what sort of "drama" those who seek to persuade us might be evoking and to consider alternatives.

Summary

Whether or not a statement is persuasive involves a number of factors other than its internal logic. Successful persuasion often depends on the psychology of the audience—that is, the audience's beliefs, values, desires, and expectations. One of the oldest theories of audience psychology is Aristotle's *Rhetoric*, written in Greek antiquity. For Aristotle, persuasion is necessary whenever any of us is faced with a choice, and the success of persuasion depends not only on the logical reasoning that the speech prompts (*logos*) but also on the effective presentation of the character of the speaker (*ethos*) and the ideology of the audience (*pathos*). We can detect *ethos, pathos,* and *logos* in many different kinds of modern-day texts—for example, political speeches, advertisements, and everyday conversation, to name just a few.

In this century, both J. L. Austin's *speech act theory* and Kenneth Burke's *dramatism* supplement Aristotle's view of persuasion and suggest that effective persuasion occurs when both speaker and audience, writer and reader, share a common *label* for what is being said. Speech act theory recognizes that every statement *performs* a certain action, such as a promise, a command, an announcement, a warning, or a guarantee. But the *performative force* of any given statement can be understood differently by different audiences. For instance, depending upon who is doing the talking and who is doing the listening, "See you later" might be understood as a promise, a threat, a request for future contact, a warning, or an act of farewell.

In a theory that complements the ideas of both Aristotle and Austin, Kenneth Burke proposes that the ways in which different audiences categorize, or label, a given statement can vary widely. This depends on how the audience understands:

1. the Act being performed
2. the Scene in which it is taking place
3. the Agent, or originator of the Act
4. the Agency, or medium, through which the Act is delivered
5. the Purpose of the Act

Burke calls these five terms his *pentad*. The Act of a seven-year-old Agent yelling (Agency) "Yabba Dabba Do" in his second-grade classroom (Scene) might be labeled "disobedience" by the teacher and understood to have disruption as its Purpose. But the same statement, yelled in the playground during recess, might be labeled "happy exuberance." The variety of reactions to the not-guilty verdict in the O. J. Simpson criminal trial allows for the construction of a number of different Burkean pentads.

❖ Questions to Ask Yourself

1. What specific statements in this chapter help establish the *ethos* of the author—that is, his practical wisdom, moral virtue, and goodwill toward the audience?

2. Is the author's *ethos* affected by the fact that he explains and adapts the theories of well-established philosophers, namely, Aristotle, Kenneth Burke, and J. L. Austin? How so?

3. Does the author rely on enthymemes to be persuasive? What about maxims? examples? Explain your answers.

4. Who is the intended audience for this chapter (or is there more than one)?

5. Do the members of this audience share certain beliefs, values, desires, and expectations? Again, explain your answers.

6. What specific statements or examples are designed to appeal to this audience?

7. What are some kinds of performatives illustrated by statements in this chapter? Here are some possibilities from which to choose:

affirm	deny	state	describe
inform	answer	object to	define
choose	warn	urge	advise
recommend	assure	favor	praise
accept	reject	simplify	complicate
emphasize	illustrate	conclude	

8. The author writes on page 31, "Aristotle's *ethos, pathos,* and *logos;* Austin's speech acts; and Burke's dramatism provide the *grammar,* or set of basic structures, with which we view persuasion in the following chapters." What sort of Act is he performing? For what Purpose?

❖ *Writing Exercise*

What are some purposes of silence? Does it have performative force? Consider, for instance:

- The White House press secretary answering a question with "No comment."

- A classroom full of students that falls silent when the teacher asks, "Any questions?"

- Vice-President Albert Gore's speech at the 1996 Democratic Convention, in which he attacked the evils of smoking but was silent about having once been a tobacco farmer.

Write a brief essay in which you consider the purposes of silence, perhaps using the above examples as guidelines but supplying examples of your own.

❖ *Persuasive Strategies for Student Writers*

Understanding how persuasion works should prompt us to consider the effectiveness of our own efforts to persuade others; to that end, we will devote some space at the conclusion of each chapter to the elements of persuasion that academic writers should keep in mind. First of all, it is important to realize that, as this chapter suggests, *all* speaking and writing entails the elements of persuasion we have reviewed, whether it is intentionally persuasive or not. In other words, all utterances (even a simple "welcome," as the example on page 15 shows) prompt us to make judgments about the character of the speaker, the motives behind the utterance, its performative force, its appropriateness and relevance to the Scene and the audience, and so forth.

We begin, then, with a set of general questions—associated with the elements of persuasion discussed so far—that any writer or collaborative group of writers might consider. These are questions that can be revisited at any stage in the writing process and indeed should be revisited several times in the course of composing an academic paper. You may want to consider these questions in connection with attempting the Writing Exercise above.

1. What statements, facts, statistics, details, experiences, or documentation demonstrate *phronesis,* or practical wisdom, about my topic? In other words, how does the writing convey *authority?*

2. Will an audience regard the interests or opinions I express as honest, well intentioned, and fair? Why or why not?

3. Do I seem to have the best interests of the audience in mind? Will they perceive me to care about, for instance, the increase of their knowledge or the improvement of some aspect of their lives? How so?

4. What is the *ideology* of my intended audience: its beliefs, values, desires, expectations? One way to address this question is to consider factors such as age, ethnicity, socioeconomic status, and education.

5. What emotional response would I like to produce: happiness? indignation? fear? confidence? uncertainty? approval? (The list of possibilities goes on.)

6. Are there any if/then sentences in my writing? (Remember that this enthymemic structure can also utilize prepositions such as *for, because,* and *since.*)

7. What shared premises have I deliberately left out of certain sentences, presuming that my audience will fill them in?

8. Are the examples I give typical or exceptional? (Note, for instance, that the description of Mrs. Lindsay in the Maytag advertisement on page 8 gives examples that portray her as a typical homemaker, thus suggesting that what is true for her will be true for other typical homemakers. Were she more exceptional—let's say, the parent of ten children—a more typical homemaker might have found her experiences less relevant.)

9. What actions would I like my writing, or parts of my writing, to perform? To begin with, consider again this list of options:

affirm	deny	state	describe
inform	answer	object to	define
choose	warn	urge	advise
recommend	assure	favor	praise
accept	reject	simplify	complicate
emphasize	illustrate	conclude	

(You might try working through one or two of your paragraphs, attempting to label the intended performative force of each sentence.)

10. Try constructing a pentad that represents the way you would like your writing to be understood. For instance, suppose you were writing on the advisability of English-only regulations:

Act:	Presenting the pros and cons of printing all U.S. government publications in English only
Scene:	A U.S. city with a diverse ethnic and racial population
Agent:	A sophomore in college who emigrated to the United States from Taiwan ten years ago with her family
Agency:	A 1,500-word essay
Purpose:	To arrive at a well-informed decision about whether English-only regulations serve the best interests of the city

If you are trying out the Writing Exercise on the purposes of silence, you might try constructing a pentad on that topic.

❖ *Preview of the Following Chapters*

Aristotle's *ethos, pathos,* and *logos;* Austin's speech acts; and Burke's dramatism provide the *grammar,* or set of basic structures, with which we view persuasion in the following chapters. In each, we will focus on a major text from one of five major arenas: the courtroom, literature, film, television, and political oratory.

In Chapter 2, we will consider the 1925 trial of John T. Scopes, who was accused of teaching theories of evolution in his public school class-room, in violation of Tennessee's Anti-Evolution Act. The trial involved major national figures, such as attorney Clarence Darrow and politician William Jennings Bryan, and attracted international attention. What worked as effective persuasion in this trial depended on elements as local as the hot July weather and as global as Bryan's presidential aspirations.

Next, in Chapter 3, we turn to nineteenth-century novelist Jane Austen and contemporary filmmaker Spike Lee. We will concentrate on Austen's *Persuasion* (1818), a novel that certainly suits our concerns here because it dramatizes the difficulty of drawing conclusions and making judgments based on how we understand what other people say. Spike Lee's *Do the Right Thing* (1989) will serve as a current example of dramatism built on dialogues between characters from different races and cultures who have different conceptions of what the "right thing" is and thus are often bent on persuading one another.

In Chapter 4, we look at the National Football League's Super Bowl, a major media event that has attracted the largest television audiences in history. The 1996 Super Bowl telecast incorporated three traditional purposes of communication: *to teach, to please,* and *to move.* Achieving these purposes through a combination of *ethos, pathos,* and *kairos* (or timeliness), the Super Bowl epitomizes much of what television pro-gramming in general has to sell.

Along with the Super Bowl, the other major persuasion event that happens every January in the United States is the State of the Union ad-dress. In Chapter 5, using the elements of persuasion explained in this book, we will analyze President Bill Clinton's 1996 address, both as a written text and as it was delivered to a national television audience. Clinton delivered this address in a particularly heated political atmos-phere, just prior to the November 1996 presidential election, in which he was a Democratic candidate and in front of a Congress in which the majority was Republican. We will ask what sorts of enthymemic, performative, and dramatistic appeals emerged as Clinton the candidate, the president, and the minority Democrat addressed the nation.

2

Persuasion in the Courtroom

The 1925 Scopes Trial

A "Duel to the Death": Background and Significance of the Scopes Trial

In July 1925, John T. Scopes was put on trial for teaching evolution in a Dayton, Tennessee, high school. He was accused of violating the Butler Act, signed into law earlier that year, which stated:

> Be it enacted by the General Assembly of the State of Tennessee that it should be unlawful for any teacher in any of the universities, normals and other public schools of the State, which are supported in whole or in part by the public school funds of the State, to teach any theory that denies the story of the divine creation of man as taught in the Bible, and to teach instead that man is descended from a lower order of animals.

The trial attracted international attention, not because of any personal interest in Scopes, who faced at most a $500 fine if convicted. From the beginning, this trial pitted two great adversaries—religious fundamentalism and academic freedom—against each other. The Butler Act was one of several state laws passed in the 1920s at the urging of Christian fundamentalist groups, who saw the growing acceptance of Darwin's theory of evolution, and its teaching in the schools, as a threat to the authority and literal meaning of the Bible. After the Butler Act passed in March 1925, the American Civil Liberties Union became interested in initiating a court case that would test the legality of the act and advertised their eagerness to provide the legal defense for a teacher willing to stand trial. Anticipating the national attention such a case would draw, several prominent citizens of Dayton, Tennessee, saw the chance to put their town on the map and asked John T. Scopes if he would be willing to stand trial. He agreed. Even though Scopes had only taught biology for two weeks that schoolyear as a substitute for the regular teacher, he had worked from a textbook that covered evolution and could reasonably be accused of violating the Butler Act.

The most prominent member of the prosecution team was William Jennings Bryan; he had volunteered to prosecute Scopes. A religious fundamentalist who had been influential in the passage of the Butler Act, Bryan was known as the "Great Crusader." He was perhaps the most famous public speaker and political figure of the time, a former presidential candidate and secretary of state who identified himself with the traditional values and interests of rural Americans. In *The Great Monkey Trial* (1968), L. Sprague De Camp quotes a speech by Bryan, in which he characterized the trial as a "duel to the death":

> The contest between evolution and Christianity is a duel to the
> death. It has been in the past a death struggle in the darkness.
> From this time on it will be a death grapple in the light. If
> evolution wins in Dayton, Christianity goes—not suddenly,
> of course, but gradually—for the two cannot stand together.
> They are as antagonistic as light and darkness, as good and
> evil. (p. 141)

The defense team was already populated by a number of distinguished lawyers, and once Bryan announced his participation, Clarence Darrow joined them. Among conservatives and fundamentalists, Darrow was as infamous as Bryan was famous. He had provided the legal defense for a number of controversial clients, beginning with a group of anarchists accused of causing a fatal bomb explosion during Chicago's Haymarket Square labor demonstration in 1886 and leading to his most sensational case prior to the Scopes trial, the 1924 defense of Nathan Leopold and Richard Loeb, who were accused of the vicious murder of a small boy. Darrow was a professed agnostic and a severe opponent of any individual or group that wanted to interfere with individual liberty. The presiding judge was John Tate Raulston of the Tennessee Circuit Court; aside from his profession, Raulston gave sermons in the Methodist Episcopal church and occasionally led religious revival meetings.

With the arrival of Bryan and Darrow on the scene in the summer of 1925, Dayton was the center of international attention. Noted American journalist and satirist H. L. Mencken, who dubbed the event the "Monkey Trial," was writing for the *Baltimore Sun*, along with reporters from all major American newspapers. Writers for the three major international news services—United Press, Associated Press, and International News Service—all had places in the courtroom when the trial began on Friday, July 10. WGN radio from Chicago was set to broadcast the proceedings live, and a public address system was in place to suit the overflow crowd waiting outside the courthouse. Food stands, tent shows, preachers, and strolling entertainers filled the streets of Dayton. The weather was terribly hot and humid, and most of the people in the packed courtroom were fanning themselves to gain some slight relief.

Day One

Oh, God, our divine Father, we recognize Thee as the Supreme Ruler of the universe.
     —Reverend Cartwright, from the opening prayer

The morning session opened with a long prayer, and the whole day was occupied mainly with empanelment of jury. The jury chosen consisted of 12 white men, mostly farmers of different Protestant religions; all but one could read. The second day, Monday, July 13, opened once again with a prayer and was then taken up with the defense motion to quash the indictment against Scopes on 13 different grounds, most of them challenging the constitutionality of the indictment and the law. The defense argued, for instance, that the Butler Act contradicted the stated duty of the Tennessee legislature to "cherish literature and science" and violated the provision that "no preference shall ever be given, by law, to any religious establishment or mode of worship." The defense asked Judge Raulston to withhold his ruling on this motion until they had presented a number of expert witnesses from the fields of science and religion. However, Raulston decided that he would rule on the motion to quash the indictment before the appearance of the defense witnesses, thereby reducing the possibility that such witnesses would actually be allowed to testify.

Day Two

It is impossible, if you leave freedom in the world, to mold the opinions of one man upon the opinions of another—only tyranny can do it.
    —Clarence Darrow, in opposition to the indictment against Scopes

Arguments for and against the motion to quash the indictment filled the day. The jury was not present, since the actual trial of Scopes had not yet begun. Darrow argued passionately for much of the afternoon that this trial was a "death struggle between two civilizations": Those who wished to prosecute Scopes represented the civilization of the sixteenth century, when people who practiced intellectual freedom were branded as witches and cruelly punished. He called instead for modern civilization to prevail, a civilization in which the rights of the individual are preserved.

Day Three

This is a God-fearing country.
    —A. T. Stewart, chief attorney for the prosecution

Darrow began the morning by objecting to the practice of opening each trial day with a prayer. Judge Raulston overruled the objection, saying, "I believe in prayer myself; I constantly invoke divine guidance myself, when I am on the bench and off the bench; I see no reason why I should not continue to do this." This day's proceedings mainly involved arguments regarding Darrow's objection and Judge Raulston's worries that journalists covering the trial were transmitting information about his rulings before he had formally announced them.

Day Four

Oh Thou to Whom all pray and for Whom are many names.
— Reverend Dr. Potter, delivering a (very brief) opening prayer

Judge Raulston read his ruling *against* the motion to quash Scopes's indictment, addressing each defense argument with an extensive formal response. In the afternoon, the trial of John Scopes finally began with the defendant's entering a plea of not guilty, followed by the opening statement by the defense, the swearing in of the jury, the presentation of the prosecution's case against Scopes, and the testimony of one scientific witness for the defense. The prosecution's case ended before the afternoon was over, with a handful of students and school officials testifying that Scopes had indeed used a biology textbook that included the theory of evolution. The single witness for the defense appearing that day was a zoologist who testified that evolution is a process widely accepted by the scientific community and that believing in evolution did not conflict with his religious practice or beliefs. This testimony was given without the jury present because the judge had not yet ruled on the admissibility of expert testimony and was hearing this witness to determine what sort of testimony would be given by the defense's team of experts.

Day Five

There is never a duel with the truth.
— Dudley Field Malone, attorney for the defense

The day was taken up with arguments for and against allowing expert scientific and religious witnesses to testify, again without the jury present. The main argument of the defense was that the wording of the Butler Act itself only incriminates "whoever teaches . . . the origin of man, contrary to that contained in the divine account of the Bible"; the wording does not *explicitly* describe evolution. Expert witnesses were needed, the defense argued, to clarify the relationship between divine creation and evolution and to show that teaching the fact of evolution does not deny the process of divine creation.

Day Six

Don't worry about us. The state of Tennessee don't rule the world yet.
　　—Clarence Darrow

Judge Raulston ruled against the admissibility of expert witnesses, prompting the above response from Darrow. Raulston decided that the intention of the law was to disallow the teaching of evolution and that determining whether Scopes did so required only "ordinary understanding" and not testimony by outside experts. Raulston did allow, however, that written versions of the experts' testimony could be included with the trial record for review when the case reached a higher court.

Day Seven

I am simply trying to protect the word of God against the greatest atheist or agnostic in the United States.
　　—William Jennings Bryan, on agreeing to be examined by
　　Clarence Darrow

The defense asked to call William Jennings Bryan as an expert witness on the Bible; astonished, Raulston turned to Bryan, who agreed to testify. Given his reputation as a fundamentalist, this was a challenge from which Bryan could not shrink. Darrow, in the face of certain defeat for his client, seemed to be trying to score a moral victory by winning this confrontation with Bryan. The testimony would be given for the record only, without the jury present. Darrow quizzed Bryan insistently about his belief that every word in the Bible should be taken literally, attempting to show that such a belief was unreasonable and illogical. Bryan admitted that the world may not have been created in seven 24-hour days. He allowed that a Biblical *day* may refer to a time period of indeterminate length. In doing so, Bryan paved the way for the belief that divine creation could have taken billions of years, consistent with the scientific theory of evolution.

Day Eight

I think to save time we will ask the court to bring in the jury and instruct
the jury to find the defendant guilty.
—Clarence Darrow

On July 21, 1925, John T. Scopes was found guilty by the jury, which deliberated only nine minutes. The verdict surprised no one, since all understood that the purpose of this trial was to make possible an appeal to the U.S. Supreme Court, which might decide the constitutionality of the Butler Act. Scopes was fined $100.

On July 26, before leaving Dayton, William Jennings Bryan died in his sleep of undetermined causes. He had just completed a written address against evolution that concluded ironically with the words "Faith of our fathers—holy faith; We will be true to thee till death!" The Scopes case was appealed to the Tennessee Supreme Court, which reversed the decision on a technicality without commenting on the constitutionality of the Butler Act. The chief justice discouraged any further legal action, saying, "We see nothing to be gained by prolonging the life of this bizarre case." The Butler Act remained on the books in Tennessee until 1967.

Aristotelian Persuasion in Court

The Bible is the Word of God; the Bible is the only expression of man's
hope of salvation. The Bible, the record of the Son of God, the Savior of
the world, born of the Virgin Mary, crucified and risen again—that
Bible is not going to be driven out of this court by experts who have come
hundreds of miles to testify that they can reconcile evolution, with its
ancestor in the jungle, or man made by God in His image and put here
for purposes as part of the divine plan. . . . The facts are simple, the case
is plain, and if those gentlemen want to enter upon a larger field of
educational work on the subject of evolution, let us get through with this
case and then convene a mock court, for it will deserve the title of mock
court if its purpose is to banish from the hearts of the people the Word of
God as revealed.
—William Jennings Bryan, for the prosecution

There is never a duel with the truth. The truth always wins and we are
not afraid of it. The truth is no coward. The truth does not need the law.
The truth does not need the forces of government. The truth does not
need Mr. Bryan. The truth is imperishable, eternal and immortal and
needs no human agency to support it. We are ready to tell the truth as
we understand it and we do not fear all the truth that they can present
as facts. [Facing William Jennings Bryan, and raising his voice] We are
ready. We are ready. We feel we stand with progress. We feel we stand
with science. We feel we stand with intelligence. We feel we stand with
fundamental freedom in America. We are not afraid. Where is the fear?
We meet it, where is the fear? We defy it, we ask your honor to admit the
evidence as a matter of correct law, as a matter of sound procedure and
as a matter of justice to the defense in this case.

   —Dudley Field Malone, for the defense

Speaking on the fifth day of the trial, William Jennings Bryan and
Dudley Field Malone each delivered impassioned pleas—Malone speaking in favor of putting expert scientific witnesses on the stand and
Bryan speaking against it. As L. Sprague De Camp reports in *The Great
Monkey Trial* (1968), Bryan's speech provoked applause that was "polite
but not enthusiastic," while Malone's speech was greeted by "the loudest,
heartiest, and longest applause of the entire trial" (pp. 327, 335). Applause, of course, is often a sign of successful persuasion. When the U.S.
president delivers the State of the Union address, news reports often
mention how many times he was interrupted by applause and how long
the applause typically lasted as measures of how persuasive or well received he was. So, we may want to ask in this instance, Why was Bryan
less persuasive than Malone? Addressing this question will prompt our
investigation of some features of Aristotelian rhetoric at work during
the Scopes trial. Given that so many of the people in the courtroom
were religious townsfolk who were suspicious of evolution and that
Scopes's guilt was, by this time, almost a foregone conclusion, their approval for Malone could not be mistaken as rooting for the defense.

Ethos

Recall that for Aristotle, the *ethos* of a speaker can contribute to the
persuasive power of a speech. *Ethos* consists of those elements of a speech
that exhibit the speaker's common sense or practical wisdom, moral

virtue, and goodwill. *Ethos* can also include the speaker's reputation. Bryan's reputation and popularity with the townsfolk of Dayton virtually guaranteed that his speech would be well received. Malone seemed to realize, however, that no such welcome would be automatic for him; in this connection, what is unusual and effective about Malone's speech is his refusal to feature his own *ethos*. Notice that he never uses *I* in this address, seeming to acknowledge that the *ethos* that will be most effective before the courtroom audience in Dayton, Tennessee, is not that of this New York Irish divorce lawyer, well known for his defense of underdogs and his support of the feminist movement. The Dayton locals who populated the courtroom—mainly conservative, middle-aged farmers—would be unlikely to see this sacrilegious political liberal as sharing their common sense or moral virtue; in fact, many would view Malone's presence in Dayton as an affront to local values, rather than any act of goodwill. Therefore, to the extent that Malone emphasized his ideas as *personal views*, he would probably be creating an *ethos* unlikely to elicit applause from this audience. But applaud they did.

Leaving aside himself as a person, Malone seems to say, "This is not *me* speaking; this is *truth* speaking." After all, he does say that truth "needs no human agency to support it." In effect, truth itself becomes the spokesperson here; the persuasive power of the speech is located not in the *ethos* of Malone but in the *ethos* of truth. Further, the repetition of *we,* while it might refer specifically to the defense team, also brings the courtroom audience into the collective group that is ready to meet truth on its own terms. By identifying himself with truth, Malone also identifies himself with an audience that believes in truth and suggests that he has common sense enough to share a general respect for truth with them.

The response by the court audience to Malone at other points in the trial was less enthusiastic. In his opening statement, Malone attempted to establish scientific knowledge as an overwhelming body of practical wisdom, thus according science itself a strong *ethos:*

> We shall prove by experts and scientists in every field of scientific knowledge that there is no branch of science which can be taught today without teaching the theory of evolution, and that this applies to geology, biology, botany, astronomy, medicine, chemistry, bacteriology, embryology, zoology, sanitation, forestry and agriculture.

There was no emotional outpouring of approval in court for statements like this, even though they were concrete and authoritative. This should have come as no surprise, however, considering that Malone was speaking to an audience of mainly farmers, who were likely to regard embryological or even agricultural research as activities far removed from getting the crops planted and the harvest in. But we must remember at moments like this a point that will be stressed further in our later discussion of dramatism: *The persuasive power of ethos always depends on what audience you have in mind.* Much of the oratory recited during the Scopes trial was directed not at the immediate audience but at the judges of the Tennessee Supreme Court, who would be reading the Dayton court transcript if the case were sent up on appeal.

Clarence Darrow understood that the *ethos* of William Jennings Bryan—his national and international reputation as a champion of the common man—was a factor not only in Dayton but in how the trial played in news reports worldwide and for judges in courts of appeal, who respected Bryan's long-standing authority. Darrow's cross-examination of Bryan on the seventh day of the trial was an attempt to weaken Bryan's *ethos.* One way that Darrow did this was by portraying Bryan as deliberately and stubbornly ignorant of basic scientific, historical, and cultural facts:

Darrow: You have never in all your life made any attempt to find out about the other peoples of the earth—how old their civilizations are—how long they had existed on the earth, have you?

Bryan: No, sir, I have been so well satisfied with the Christian religion that I have spent no time trying to find arguments against it. . . .

Bryan: I have all the information I want to live by and to die by.

Darrow: And that's all you are interested in?

Bryan: I am not looking for any more on religion.

Darrow: You don't care how old the earth is, how old man is and how long the animals have been here?

Bryan: I am not so much interested in that.

Darrow: You have never made any investigation to find out?

Bryan: No, sir, I have never.

Here, Bryan maintains the *ethos* of a fundamentalist, sticking with the brand of moral virtue that has defined his life and reputation. In face-offs such as this, Darrow and Bryan represent dueling *ethoi:* two brands of practical wisdom, one informed by science and the other inspired by faith; two brands of moral virtue, one based on intellectual freedom and the other on religious authority; and two brands of goodwill, one directed at communities that embrace scientific progress, the other at communities that look to the Bible as the final word.

Pathos

As Aristotle has shown, certain beliefs, values, desires, and expectations govern the emotions and states of mind of an audience. A modern persuasion theorist, Chaim Perelman, has noted that "[t]o adapt to an audience is, above all, to choose as premises of argumentation theses the audience already holds." Certainly, the loud applause for Malone's speech was a strong indication that the audience was feeling positive about what he had said. We can then ask, What *theses* does he put forward that arouse their approval? One way to answer this question is to list the general terms in Malone's speech that he stands behind: truth, courage, progress, science, intelligence, freedom, and justice.

As suggested earlier, Malone is declaring in his speech a love of truth; further, he is asking that both the prosecution and the defense get an equal chance to present their witnesses, so that the truth will emerge. With this speech, Malone echoes a principle of persuasion that Aristotle supported: If two sides of an issue are equally well represented and equally well argued, truth or right will win the day. Malone is asking that Judge Raulston make sure that this "duel to the death" is a fair fight. In a fair fight, neither the defense nor the prosecution will win but rather the truth will: "The truth always wins and we are not afraid of it."

Appealing to the audience's belief that the truth is "imperishable, eternal, and immortal," Malone also suggests that given the opportunity, humans will choose the true over the false. In this regard, he also follows Aristotle, who says that "humans have a natural disposition for the true and to a large extent hit on the truth." Malone is asking the judge to let the jury display this natural disposition by allowing the defense to present its full case. The idea that people know the truth when they hear it is one way of deflecting a common fear regarding persuasion: that a powerfully persuasive speaker can fool an audience, leading them away from truth and toward the wrong decision.

Whether this fear of being fooled is well founded is not clear, even today. As scientific and technological knowledge increases at an enormous rate, there is still no sure way to determine whether a person is speaking the truth or reconstructing an event exactly as it happened. (We've all heard the example of four different people on four different street corners who witness the same traffic accident and give four very different accounts of what happened.) So, one way to deal with the question of whether the truth will prevail, even in the midst of conflicting accounts of what happened, is simply to *believe* that it will. Malone is appealing to that belief.

Of course, the appeal to truth can have a powerful persuasive force for any number of individuals in an audience. Everyone would agree, in general, that truth is a good thing; however, it is also the case that truth is often so vague a concept that everyone can define it according to their own biases.

Judging the Truth.   Aristotle said that "humans have a natural disposition for the true," and he would be right, if people actually made choices and weighed evidence in a vacuum, where universal conceptions of truth or justice or right and wrong are in place. But that is never what happens. Each individual always brings his or her partiality along, which Aristotle himself admitted in talking about the nature of judges, saying that they do not judge objectively but are instead "considering the matter in relation to their own affairs and listening with partiality." This is quite evident in the Scopes trial when Judge Raulston overrules the defense objection to opening each court session with a prayer, saying, "I believe in prayer myself; I constantly invoke divine guidance myself, when I am on the bench and off the bench; I see no reason why I should not continue to do this."

For Aristotle, a judge is anyone in the position of determining the truth value of a statement; consider, for instance, the reader of the famous first sentences of Jane Austen's *Pride and Prejudice* (1813):

> It is a truth universally acknowledged, that a single man in possession of a good fortune, must be in want of a wife.

> However little known the feelings or views of such a man
> may be on his first entering a neighbourhood, this truth is so
> well fixed in the minds of the surrounding families, that he is
> considered as the rightful property of some one or other of their
> daughters.

The "truth universally acknowledged" is presented for our judgment. Does everyone believe that a man of good economic means wants a wife? In the next paragraph, we find that this truth is fixed in the minds of the middle-class families of an English country neighborhood, who don't really know how such a man actually feels but hold onto this truth because they want their daughters to marry well.

With these first sentences, Austen tells us that a truth we consider universal is probably only shared by people like us—those who live in the same neighborhood and share the same social class, national origin, customs, and needs. (In other words, she means "truth universally acknowledged" *ironically;* she is really saying that this truth is not universal at all.) Further, the belief in such a truth is often not the result of hard evidence. The people in Austen's neighborhood *presume* what a single man must feel without knowing that for sure. Rather, their belief is often the result of certain motives. These people want to marry off their daughters and therefore construct a truth that allows for this.

For Austen, as for Aristotle, judging claims of truth is not restricted to the courtroom. We are all judges when faced with statements as diverse as a proposition in a novel, a weather report, a "sound bite" from a political candidate, or a Doritos commercial. And as judges, we are all partial, marking as the truth a proposition that may speak to our needs and desires, and the needs and desires of people like us, but that is not at all universally acknowledged.

None of the people who were cheering wildly at the conclusion of Malone's speech were impartial judges; rather, they were all cheering for *their own version* of each of the main terms in Malone's address: truth, courage, progress, science, intelligence, freedom, and justice. As the Greek philosopher Plato, one of Aristotle's teachers, demonstrates in a dialogue called the *Phaedrus,* the word *love* functions in this way, as well: One of the most famous speakers in ancient Greece, Lysias, comes to Athens to speak on love and the nature of the lover and gains approval for what he says while never defining what *love* means. As a kind of modern-day Lysias, singer Diana Ross had a stadium full of tens of thousands of people singing, swaying, cheering, and applauding as she sang "What the World Needs Now Is Love, Sweet Love" during the half-time show of the 1996 Super Bowl. As we will note in Chapter 5, during the 1996 State of the Union address, both Republicans and Democrats applauded when President Clinton promised the end of big government, even though both sides have very different political philosophies and economic agendas. But since *big government* is not specifically defined in that speech, it invites all-purpose approval.

Logos

The courtroom audience displayed less enthusiasm for Bryan's fifth-day speech than for Malone's. Those who had expected the William Jennings Bryan of legend, the orator renowned for his keen intellectual and vocal power, saw here an aging man whose powers had diminished. Before delivering the concluding words quoted earlier, Bryan made a number of small mistakes, calling a witness named *Robinson Robertson* and forgetting altogether the name of another key witness. Bryan allowed himself to be interrupted and queried by the defense at points when his address might have been gathering strength, and his voice quavered. In terms of *ethos,* then, Bryan did not live up to his reputation; in terms of *pathos,* he did not meet the audience's desires and expectations.

Remember that *ethos* and *pathos* are elements of persuasion that are often materialized through the words of the speech, its *logos.* Bryan's speech suffers from what Aristotle calls "frigidities" of style—that is, expressions that do not engage the audience. One kind of frigidity results from telling the audience what they already know. Doing so is damaging because persuasion depends so much on audience participation, on an audience feeling that they are intellectually involved, making connections and discoveries and drawing conclusions. To the extent that a speaker is doing their thinking for them or repeating what's familiar, the audience may remain detached and passive.

When Bryan says "The Bible is the Word of God" and identifies "the Son of God, the Savior of the world, born of the Virgin Mary, crucified and risen again," he is repeating concepts and phrases that had been heard again and again, Sunday after Sunday, by this audience of regular churchgoers. Further, he concludes the speech with an overdetermined enthymeme:

> If those gentlemen want to enter upon a larger field of educational work on the subject of evolution, [then] let us get through with this case and then convene a mock court, for it will deserve the title of mock court if its purpose is to banish from the hearts of the people the word of God as revealed.

The if/then structure signals a potential enthymeme here—that is, a logical syllogism with one of its parts unexpressed, a part that the audience fills in. The enthymeme attempted here might be expressed as: "If the defense wants to educate us about evolution, then we should convene a mock court." The unexpressed premise that an audience could fill in might be: "Evolution education is a mockery of justice." But Bryan does not leave his enthymeme alone and allow his audience to complete it. Instead, he adds words to this effect: "Banishing the word of god [through evolution education] is a mockery of justice." In short, he does the audience's thinking for them, providing what they might have filled in for themselves.

In contrast to the relatively long and intellectually taxing sentences that characterize the Bryan passage, Malone relies on briefer, more rhythmic—and thus more pleasant, comprehensible, and entertaining—statements. Where Bryan gives us a frigid metaphor, Malone gives us a live one: "The truth is no coward." With this, he follows Aristotle's advice that an effective metaphor—one that gets the audience pleasantly involved—contains terms whose relationship is neither too farfetched nor too familiar or apparent. A metaphor such as "The truth is no theorem" contains terms that would be difficult for many audiences to grasp; a metaphor such as "The truth is no lie" presents the audience with no opportunity for discovering a fresh connection. Malone pitches his metaphor between these kinds of extremes.

Also, Malone's speech makes good use of the classical technique known as *anaphora*, which is the deliberate repetition of a word or phrase at the beginnings of successive statements. One of the most well-known and famous modern-day uses of anaphora is Martin Luther King, Jr.'s, repetition of "I have a dream" in the speech that has come to be known through that phrase. Malone's repetition of "We are ready" and "We feel" calls attention to the speech as speech, as a text carefully crafted by a skilled writer; in this way, the *logos* of the speech contributes to the positive appeal of Malone's *ethos*. Further, rhythmic repetition has an engaging, emotional effect, strangely magical in its ability to charm audiences.

Hillary Rodham Clinton employed *anaphora* in her September 1995 address to the United Nations Fourth World Conference on Women in Beijing, China. In the following excerpt, she emphasizes that *women's* rights cannot be considered as anything other than basic *human* rights:

> It is a violation of *human* rights when babies are denied food, or drowned, or suffocated, or their spines broken, simply because they are born girls.
>
> It is a violation of *human* rights when women and girls are sold into the slavery of prostitution.
>
> It is a violation of *human* rights when individual women are doused with gasoline, set on fire and burned to death because their marriage dowries are deemed too small.
>
> It is a violation of *human* rights when individual women are raped in their own communities and when thousands of women are subjected to rape as a tactic or prize of war.
>
> It is a violation of *human* rights when a leading cause of death worldwide among women ages 14 to 44 is the violence they are subjected to in their own homes.
>
> It is a violation of *human* rights when young girls are brutalized by the painful and degrading practice of genital mutilation.
>
> It is a violation of *human* rights when women are denied the right to plan their own families, and that includes being forced to have abortions or being sterilized against their will.
>
> If there is one message that echoes forth from this conference, it is that human rights are women's rights. And women's rights are human rights.

In this passage, Hillary Rodham Clinton conveys a powerful *ethos*, that of a world figure with a full command of the facts and examples that illustrate her common sense. She appeals to the *pathos* of an international gathering of women from countries where the offenses she lists are committed, and she does this through a *logos* that maintains its central enthymeme—"Since women are human, then crimes against women are crimes against humanity"—through the emotional emphasis that *anaphora* provides.

Speech Acts: Intentions and Interpretations

> *There is an intention every time a man does an act. You have to show the intention whether it is plain or ambiguous. You must always show the intention, that is the first thing you come to.*
> —A. T. Stewart, for the prosecution

Whenever we interpret a speech act, we take account of its probable *intention*. Disagreements about what a statement means often center on different accounts of its intention. Linguist Deborah Tannen writes about a woman who often begins statements to her mate with "Let's"—for instance, "Let's clean up now, before we start lunch." Her mate interprets statements like this as orders, but the speaker insists that they are suggestions. Tannen points out that men are typically sensitive to statements by women that seem to threaten their independence; moreover, a man will interpret instances in which a woman feels she is trying to establish cooperation and mutual pleasure (as in the statement quoted above) as attempts to push him around. Tannen's discussion, focusing on the different conversational styles and expectations of men and women, illustrates the fact that a statement never carries a particular intention independent of the situation in which it is uttered and the psychology of the individuals who are involved.

Establishing intention has powerful persuasive force. In the United States legal system, someone's intention during the commission of a crime can make the difference between a death sentence (in the case of premeditated murder) and one much less severe (in the case of, for instance, self-defense). This fact alone indicates how focused Americans are as a society on the intentions behind human actions. Apart from the intention of a criminal, the interpretation of the law itself has often addressed the question of intention; for instance, recent debates on the legality of gun control have raised the question of what the 1787 framers of the Constitution intended when they established the "right to keep and bear arms." Those who believe that we should not be persuaded by an interpretation based on some original intention say that (1) any intention that may have been operating in another era may not be relevant to current circumstances and (2) that intention can never be established with any certainty. Some psychologists propose, for instance, that everything we say or do is the result of unconscious motives and intentions.

Much of the Scopes trial focused on what the Butler Act intended and whether its intention could be established at all. The question came down to this: Did the framers of the Butler Act intend to prohibit the teaching of evolution (a word that is never mentioned in the act) or instead to prohibit only "teaching any theory that denies the story of divine creation"? Put another way, did the framers of the Butler Act intend to prohibit the teaching of evolution only if it is true that evolution denies divine creation? The defense argued that the intention of the act was not clear because the title or caption of the act was not consistent with its body. As Clarence Darrow explained:

> The caption of this act, as has been so often said, is entitled, "An act to prevent the teaching of evolution in public schools." The body of the act says: "Whoever teaches any doctrine as to the origin of man, contrary to that contained in the divine account in the Bible, and that he descended from some lower organism, is guilty," and so on. Now then, in order to make your act constitutional, the court must hold that the body of the act describes evolution.

Darrow raised this question as part of his plea that expert scientific witnesses be allowed to testify for the defense. He proposed that such witnesses could establish that the theory of evolution does not contradict a belief in divine creation: If the body of the act never mentions evolution and if evolution can be shown to allow for divine creation, then Scopes's teaching evolution is not a violation of the act.

Establishing the meaning and applicability of the act finally came down to determining the *intention* of the legislature, as A. T. Stewart argued for the prosecution:

> The cardinal rule of construction in Tennessee, as I stated, your honor, is that the intention of the legislature shall govern your honor in construing the statute. Do you suppose, your honor, that the legislature intended to open the doors to an unending and everlasting argument about whether there is a conflict? Did they have such a thought in mind? How could they? How could the legislature of this state, a body of such splendid men, as we had there last year—how could they design such a thought—how could they hope to place upon the people of this commonwealth such a dangerous law?

Here, Stewart appealed to the *ethos* of the legislature, suggesting that they were men of good common sense who would not intentionally design a law that opened up the possibility of Darrow's interpretation. The prosecution argued further that the framers of the law did not intend it to require interpretation from expert witnesses and that the defense's argument for experts implied that the local members of the jury were stupid. As Sue Hicks of the prosecution said, "If they want to make a school down here to educate our poor ignorant people, let them establish a school out here; let them bring in their great experts." This was an appeal to the *pathos* of the local audience, maintaining the defense team as elitist outsiders who don't understand or appreciate the minds and hearts of Dayton folk. In these instances, we see Aristotelian appeals being utilized in the service of establishing the illocutionary force of a speech act, namely, the intention of the Butler Act. For the prosecution, the Butler Act clearly intends to prohibit the teaching of evolution and is not open to alternate interpretations.

Judge Raulston ruled against the defense, stating that "the legislative intent will prevail" and adding that "the ordinary, non-expert mind can comprehend the simple language [of the Butler Act]." Because the law clearly prohibited the teaching of evolution, "then the evidence of experts would shed no light on the issues."

The Dramatistic Bible

*What is the Bible? Different sects of Christians disagree in their answers
to this question. . . . The various Protestant sects of Christians use the
King James version, published in London in 1611, while Catholics use
the Douay version, of which the Old Testament was published by the
English college at Douay, in France, in 1609, and the New Testament by
the English college at Rheims in 1582, and these two versions are often
called, respectively, the Protestant Bible and the Catholic Bible. The
original manuscripts, containing the inspired word of God, written in
Hebrew, in Aramaic and in Greek, have all been lost for many hundreds
of years, and each of the Bibles mentioned is a translation, not of those
manuscripts, but of translations thereof into the Greek and Latin. The
earliest copy of the Old Testament in Hebrew now in existence was
made as late as the eleventh century, though there are partial copies
made in the ninth and tenth centuries. The oldest known Greek
manuscripts of the Bible, except a few fragments, belong to the fourth
and fifth centuries. Each party claims for its own version the most
accurate presentation of the inspired word as delivered to mankind and
contained in the original scriptures.*

*Which version does the Tennessee legislature call for? Does it intend
to distinguish between the different religious sects in passing this law?
Does it mean the Protestant, the [King] James version, rather than the
Catholic or Douay Bible? . . . You know there is a Hebrew Bible, of some
thirty-nine books; and there is a Protestant Bible, and a Catholic
Bible—the Protestant of sixty-six and the Catholic of eighty books; and
you have the King James version, and a revised version and there are
30,000 differences between the King James version and it. You have the
King James version here; there are thousands of Bibles.*

—Arthur G. Hays, for the defense

On the fourth day of the Scopes trial, the defense focused on *the
Bible* as a key term in the Butler Act, especially because it was the teachings of the Bible that Scopes was accused of violating. In terms of Kenneth Burke's dramatism, the Bible becomes the Scene for Scopes's Act: It
is the text that sets forth the story of creation that the Butler Act wants
to maintain as the "primal scene" for all of us, that is, the beginning of
humankind. With reference to the wording of the Butler Act, denying

"the story of divine creation" becomes an illegal Act, and the Agent is John Scopes. The Agency of his violation is teaching, and his Purpose—though never explicitly stated—is implied by William Jennings Bryan when he refers to the general purpose of the defense, Scopes included, as banishing "the Word of God as revealed."

The Burkean pentad that results from this identification of the Bible as the Scene looks like this:

Scene: The Bible

Act: Denying the story of divine creation

Agent: John T. Scopes

Agency: Teaching

Purpose: "Banish . . . the Word of God as revealed"

As we saw in the discussion of the O. J. Simpson trial in Chapter 1, changing or redefining one term in the pentad affects all the others. In the Scopes trial, the defense sought to change the force and meaning of the Butler Act by proposing that teaching theories of evolution is not inconsistent with the creation story in the Bible. One way to make this case, in addition to those we have already discussed, is to take issue with the nature of the Scene in which this Act occurred. Redefining the Scene changes the nature of the Act.

Asking "What is the Bible?" defense attorney Arthur Hays quoted from a previous court case in order to complicate and challenge the prosecution's assertion that the King James version was the one "in common use." By enumerating the long history of production of different versions of the Bible, Hays tried to change what Kenneth Burke would call the *scope* and *circumference* of the term *the Bible*. Burke says this in *A Grammar of Motives* about *scope:*

> [People] seek for vocabularies that will be faithful *reflections* of reality. To this end, they must develop vocabularies that are *selections* of reality. And any selection of reality must, in certain circumstances, function as a *deflection* of reality. Insofar as the vocabulary meets the needs of reflection, we can say that it has the necessary scope. (1969, p. 59)

Hays is arguing that the term *the Bible* should be defined to fully reflect the reality of many different versions of the Bible. To the extent that *the Bible* is restricted to meaning the King James version only, Hays suggests, it is merely a narrow *selection* of reality and thereby functions as a *deflection,* or refusal, of reality.

   Circumference, for Burke, refers to the size and limits of one's scope. We can say that Hays is proposing a broader scope and a larger circumference for the definition of *the Bible.* For Burke, then, *scope* and *circumference* refer to how inclusive a term is. If among all the foods available, I like only the tastes of chocolate ice cream and pepperoni pizza, the scope and circumference of good taste (as it applies to food) are severely limited for me—certainly only a narrow *selection* of what is available and a *deflection* of the reality that many other options exist. If, on the other hand, I never eat the same food twice in the same month and enjoy everything I eat, the scope and circumference of my good taste are considerably more inclusive.

   In an introductory literature class I taught, a student once asked me why we were reading poems by Emily Dickinson, plays by Shakespeare, and a novel by Ernest Hemingway; as far as he was concerned, literature should be for entertainment, not analysis. (He mentioned some Western and science fiction novels as favorites that he'd prefer.) Another student in the same class objected to the literature I had chosen as too exclusively traditional and wondered why we weren't reading works by non-white, non-Western authors whose literature was more representative of the multicultural and multiethnic student body. Taken together, these two students and I engaged the very important question of the scope and circumference of the term *literature.*

   In Plato's *Phaedrus,* mentioned earlier, Socrates tells the student Phaedrus that in order for two people to learn from one another in an exchange, they must share a working definition of the term they are discussing. (In the case of this dialogue, the term is *love.*) So, arriving at an agreeable definition, which entails for both parties the same scope and circumference, is crucial. On Day Four of the Scopes trial, the Reverend Potter responded to the defense's objection to an opening prayer by making his prayer short and beginning with "Oh Thou to Whom all pray and for Whom are many names." With these words, he is trying to expand the scope and circumference of names for *God* in an effort to make the prayer more acceptable to a larger number of people. Hays, in his speech, wants to expand the scope and circumference of *the Bible* in a way that the prosecution could not possibly find agreeable. Pressing them to define this term precisely and broadly—taking into account the many different books in different languages that have been called *the Bible* through the ages—Hays discredits the Butler Act because it does not define precisely what Scopes is accused of violating. In sum, if the Scene for Scopes's Act becomes the many Bibles that have existed in different cultures and religions and historical eras, then the nature of the alleged crime takes on, in effect, too much scope and circumference to prosecute.

Clarence Darrow tried to further complicate the scope and circumference of *the Bible* in his examination of William Jennings Bryan. Darrow tried to get Bryan to clarify what periods of time the Book of Genesis refers to with the word *day:*

Darrow: Does the statement, "The morning and the evening were the first day," and "The morning and the evening were the second day," mean anything to you?

Bryan: I do not think it necessarily means a twenty-four-hour day. . . .

Darrow: Then, when the Bible said, for instance, "and God called the firmament heaven. And the evening and the morning were the second day," that does not necessarily mean twenty-four hours?"

Bryan: I do not think it necessarily does.

Darrow: Do you think it does or does not?

Bryan: I know a great many think so.

Darrow: What do you think?

Bryan: I do not think it does.

Darrow: You think those were not literal days?

Bryan: I do not think they were twenty-four hour days. . . . But I think it would be just as easy for the kind of God we believe in to make the earth in six days as in six years or in 6,000,000 years or in 600,000,000 years. I do not think it important whether we believe one or the other.

Darrow: Do you think those were literal days?

Bryan: My impression is they were periods, but I would not attempt to argue as against anybody who wanted to believe in literal days.

Darrow: Have you any idea of the length of the periods?

Bryan: No, I don't.

Darrow: Do you think the sun was made on the fourth day?

Bryan: Yes.

Darrow: And they had evening and morning without the sun?

Bryan: I am simply saying it is a period.

Darrow: They had evening and morning for four periods without the sun, do you think?

Bryan: I believe in creation as there told, and if I am not able to explain it I will accept it. Then you can explain it to suit yourself. . . .

Darrow: Do you believe, whether it was a literal day or a period, the sun and the moon were not made until the fourth day?

Bryan: I believe they were made in the order in which they were given there. . . . I believe that it was made on the fourth day, in the fourth day.

Darrow: And they had the evening and the morning before that time for three days or three periods. All right, that settles it. Now, if you call those periods, they may have been a very long time.

Bryan: They might have been.

Darrow: The creation might have been going on for a very long time?

Bryan: It might have continued for millions of years.

Here Darrow emphasizes the Scene of creation, as stated in the King James Bible, as a series of *days*. At issue is whether "the story of divine creation," as stated in the Bible and referred to in the Butler Act, can refer to a series of days that could have provided enough time for evolution. If a *day* can be admitted to have broad scope and circumference, then it can be argued that evolution is the Agency for divine creation because the creation of human life may have evolved over the course of a day lasting millions of years.

In general, enlarging the scope and circumference of a term will make it more agreeable to more people. That was clearly the result when the term *freedom* was enlarged in the United States to include people who had been slaves and the term *voter* was enlarged by the Nineteenth Amendment to the Constitution (passed in 1920), giving women the right to vote.

Darrow's examination of Bryan had no legal consequences in the Scopes trial. The jury was not allowed to be present, and the Darrow-Bryan exchange was not even included in the court record that went forward to the court of appeals. But it was reported widely in national and international newspapers and was effective as Aristotelian *pathos* insofar as it evoked a number of expressions of pity for Bryan, who clearly seemed past his prime.

A recent court case in Tennessee illustrates how elements that had one kind of effect in the Scopes trial can have quite another today. In March 1991, Brittney Settle—a ninth-grade student at a public school in Dickson, Tennessee—was assigned, along with her classmates, to write a research paper on a topic of her choice, to be approved by the teacher, Dana Ramsey. Settle, a practicing Christian, proposed to write on "The Life of Jesus Christ." Ramsey would not approve this topic, noting that Settle's strong Christian beliefs and background would not allow her to learn about a new, unfamiliar topic or to conduct objective research. Ramsey also explained that criticizing Settle's writing on this topic—for instance, grammar or organization—could be misunderstood as criticism of her personal beliefs. Despite her teacher's disapproval, Settle wrote the paper and received a failing grade.

Settle sued the Dickson County School Board to have the failing grade removed from her record and to receive damages. Her attorneys argued that a public school may "not censor or punish individual student expression . . . on the basis of its particular religious viewpoint," calling this a case of "viewpoint discrimination." However, the school board won in federal court and in the U.S. Court of Appeals, and in November 1995, the U.S. Supreme Court refused without comment to hear Settle's appeal of these decisions. The appeals court said, "Teachers . . . must be given broad discretion to give grades and conduct class discussion based on the content of speech. Learning is more vital in the class-room than free speech."

Compare this last sentence to Bryan's comment about John Scopes's right to free speech. He said, "Mr. Scopes has the right to say anything he wants except in the schoolroom where he is an employee of the State." Scopes's attorneys, like Settle's, argued repeatedly that he was being deprived of his right to free speech. And in both cases, the circumference of free speech does not include the public school classroom. In Settle's case, however, the issue was religious content, and in Scopes's case, secular content. Even so, if we think of the two cases in terms of Burke's pentad, there are striking general similarities:

The Settle Case, 1991–1995

Scene:	Tennessee public school
Act:	Prohibition of expression in the classroom
Agent:	The state and its educational institutions
Agency:	Failing grade

The Scopes Case, 1925

Scene:	Tennessee public school
Act:	Prohibition of expression in the classroom
Agent:	The state and its educational institutions
Agency:	Criminal prosecution

Certainly, the Agency, or means of prohibition, seems much more severe in the case of Scopes than that of Settle. However, the trial and Scopes's notoriety actually led to him receiving a scholarship for graduate study in geology at the University of Chicago, which led to a long, successful career. The significant difference between these two cases is not Agency, but Purpose.

In the Settle case, the teacher's purpose for prohibiting the topic "The Life of Jesus Christ," a purpose supported by the school's curriculum and goals, may be expressed as "Encouraging learning of the unfamiliar." One specific requirement of this paper was that each student write on an unfamiliar topic, thereby implying that learning itself involves confronting new information and ideas. By contrast, the purpose of prohibiting the teaching of evolution in Tennessee in 1925 was "Conserving the familiar," identifying school learning with the reiteration of long-established, prevailing religious beliefs. And in March 1996, the Tennessee Senate considered new legislation that would once again prohibit teaching evolution. The Evolution Bill, as it was called, failed to pass, with 13 in favor and 20 opposed. Such recent cases show us that definitions of *learning* continue to be under debate; our concluding observation here is that the definition of *learning* itself remains a key element of persuasion.

Summary

In July 1925, John T. Scopes stood trial for violating Tennessee's Butler Act, which prohibited the teaching of evolution. Two famous orators and social activists, William Jennings Bryan and Clarence Darrow, held prominent positions on the prosecution team (Bryan) and the defense team (Darrow). Each team represented a very different *ethos:* The prosecution defined its practical wisdom, moral virtue, and goodwill with reference to religious authority and the teachings of the Bible; the defense, by contrast, stressed the importance of academic freedom and scientific truth.

An appeal to *pathos* can often entail the strategic use of general, abstract terms. In a major speech, Dudley Field Malone of the defense employed such a term, *truth,* in order to utilize an important general belief on the part of the audienc—namely, that the truth of any case will be apparent if all the available evidence is presented. This is a belief that many people hold even now. But in fact, as Aristotle points out, it is not possible for anyone to define or judge the truth impartially. Moreover, what counts as truth varies from person to person; that is, even though a group of diverse individuals might agree that truth is good, they are likely to disagree about the particular truth of a specific statement. What an individual accepts as the truth will often depend on his or her needs and desires: "Carrots taste good" is truer for someone who is hungry than for someone who is full.

Malone's major speech during the trial received more enthusiastic applause than Bryan's major speech; the response of the courtroom audience to each man can be tied to the *logos* of his speech. Bryan repeated phrases and ideas that were already very familiar to the audience, so the speech did not strike them as fresh or engaging. Malone employed metaphors that were neither too familiar nor too farfetched, which helped keep the audience alert and engaged. Further, Malone relied on *anaphora,* the rhythmic repetition of key phrases that can help charm an audience.

The attorneys questioned the nature of the Butler Act as a speech act by arguing over its intention. The general questions underlying their debate were (1) whether the intended meaning or application of a law or any statement can be fixed with reference to all cases and (2) whether the original intention is relevant at all.

The defense contended that the very definition of *the Bible* was at issue in this trial. The prosecution used the King James Bible as its authority for the story of divine creation, and the defense insisted that there had been many translations and versions of the Bible, so that no one version could stand as a legal authority. With this argument, the defense brought up what Kenneth Burke would call the *scope* and *circumference* of the term *the Bible.* The greater the scope and circumference of a term, the more possible meanings it includes. Defining *the Bible* as "the King James Bible" gives it a more narrow scope and smaller circumference than defining it as "any book regarded as authoritative or official," which is one of the definitions given in *Webster's Dictionary.* Greater scope and circumference can lead to vagueness but may also make a term more agreeable or relevant to a larger audience.

❖ *Questions to Ask Yourself*

1. The author finds it best to begin this chapter with a summary of the Scopes trial and its context. What does his decision to do so imply about the nature of the audience?

2. How would you characterize the quotations from the trial that precede each day-by-day summary:
   - Contributions to the *ethos* of the author?
   - Appeals to the *pathos* of the audience?
   - Performative speech acts? (If so, what sort of act is each quotation performing?)

3. Does this chapter reveal any biases on the part of the author concerning the issues raised in the Scopes trial? That is, are there statements or sections that favor the prosecution over the defense, or vice versa? Explain your answer.

4. What purposes does Hillary Rodham Clinton's speech serve in this chapter, other than illustrating anaphora?

❖ *Writing Exercise*

In 1953, theorist Richard Weaver proposed that certain general terms hold such value that they will meet with approval from any audience; some of those he cites are *progress, fact, science, modern,* and *efficient.* An argument will tend to be persuasive, he suggests, when it uses terms like these in much the same way that Dudley Field Malone used *truth.*

Write an essay in which you consider whether any of the terms that Weaver offers are still appealing for a wide range of audiences today. Try to explain why several different audiences would respond positively to the same general term, taking into account their respective beliefs, desires, and values. If some or all of the terms that Weaver offers are no longer effective, are there others that have taken their place?

❖ *Persuasive Strategies for Student Writers*

Once again, what follows is a set of questions connected to the points covered in this chapter, to which you can refer as you compose or revise an academic paper. The questions are designed to prompt you to think about the elements of persuasion in your own writing.

1. If your writing were delivered as a public address, at what points would your audience be most likely to applaud?

2. Will the audience be able to detect any of your personal characteristics from any parts of your writing? Would indications of your personal identity make the writing *more* engaging or persuasive or *less*? How so?

3. Which of the two first-person pronouns do you rely on more heavily: *I* or *We?*

4. Are you able to include any facts or examples that will speak for themselves (in other words, facts or examples that seem to possess their own *ethos*)?

5. In *A Grammar of Motives* (1945, p. 503), Kenneth Burke says this about metaphor: "Metaphor is a device for seeing something *in terms of* something else. It brings out the thisness of a that, or the thatness of a this." When Shakespeare says "All the world's a stage," he's defining a *this* (*the world*) in terms of a *that* (*a stage*). The relationship is similar when Dudley Field Malone said, "The truth (*this*) is no coward (*that*)." Does your writing contain any "*this* is *that*" statements? If so, will your audience find your connection between *this* and *that* familiar, farfetched, or fresh? Why?

6. Which sentences express or suggest your intention? Does your intention change during the course of the writing? In other words, does the writing embody more than one intention?

3

Neighborhood Persuasions

Jane Austen and Spike Lee

Because novelists and filmmakers so often tell stories that portray conversation and conflict, they necessarily illustrate the complexities of persuasion in action. Nineteenth-century novelist Jane Austen and contemporary filmmaker Spike Lee are artists who are most concerned with whether and how persuasion works in everyday life. As Austen said, her novels all concern "3 or 4 families in a Country Village," trying to sort out their relationships with one another. Austen examines how people get along in society, and her novel *Persuasion* (1818) is particularly concerned with how 27-year-old Anne Elliot deals with her own susceptibility to persuasion. Spike Lee is also consistently concerned with how people get along in society, but instead of focusing on the psychology of the comfortable British middle class, as Austen does, Lee's film *Do the Right Thing* (1989) studies how persuasion operates along racial and social divides in a neighborhood in which whites, blacks, Hispanics, and Asians are in conversation and conflict all day, every day.

Jane Austen's *Persuasion*

It is 1814. Sir Walter Elliot is a baronet (in the ranks of British nobility, one step lower than a baron and one step higher than a knight) with three daughters: Mary, 23; Anne, 27; and Elizabeth, 29. Without the discipline exerted by his late wife, Sir Walter has squandered his money and finds himself unable to maintain his estate; he is unwilling, however, to give up any of the comforts that have run him into debt. Forced to rent the estate, Sir Walter lets it to Admiral Croft of the British Navy and his wife. Mrs. Croft, it turns out, is the sister of navy captain Frederick Wentworth, who once proposed to Anne Elliot. Anne refused him, persuaded by her friend and advisor, Lady Russell, that Wentworth was a bad choice.

When the Crofts take over the Elliot estate in Somersetshire, Sir Walter and Elizabeth leave to take residence in the city of Bath, while Anne stays in the neighborhood to tend to her ill sister, Mary. Mary is not actually very ill at all but likes the attention, it seems. Mary is the one Elliot sister who has married, to country gentleman Charles Musgrove, and they live on the Musgrove estate at Uppercross.

Captain Frederick Wentworth enters the picture. In the neighborhood to see his sister, he soon becomes acquainted with the Musgroves, as well. Inevitably, he once again meets Anne, his former love interest, but not a word passes between them about their previous relationship. Rumors develop that Wentworth is courting one of Charles Musgrove's sisters, and there is a great buzz about whether he favors Henrietta or Louisa. Anne is confused about what she should feel, and does feel, for Wentworth.

Her confusion continues when she accompanies Wentworth, Louisa, Henrietta, Mary, and Charles to the seaside to visit Wentworth's old navy companion, Captain Harville. There, they also meet Captain Benwick, who has recently lost his fiancée and is in mourning for her. Anne spends an evening having a most agreeable talk with Benwick, and there is some sense that they may be attracted to one another.

The next day, Louisa falls and hits her head. Unconscious, she remains with the Harvilles. Wentworth takes Anne and Henrietta back to Uppercross and then returns to the Harvilles and Louisa. Soon after, Anne joins her father and older sister at Bath. The question of who is courting whom becomes more complicated when William Elliot arrives at Bath. This Elliot is the nephew of Sir Walter and destined to become heir to the Elliot estate. But some years back, he insulted Sir Walter and seemed to want to have nothing to do with the family. Now he is back and seems quite attracted to Anne.

News arrives that Captain Benwick, not Wentworth, will be marrying Louisa! Soon after, Anne runs into Wentworth himself, who confirms that he was never attracted to Louisa. At Bath, Anne begins visiting a former schoolfellow of hers, Mrs. Smith, who is ill and poor but a very keen observer of local society. Mrs. Smith suspects that Anne is to become engaged to William Elliot, which Anne denies. Convinced that Anne is not in love with William Elliot, Mrs. Smith reveals Elliot's sordid history of deceit and betrayal, proving to Anne that he is merely a heartless opportunist.

The climactic scene at Bath finds Anne in a busy gathering of family friends and acquaintances, including Wentworth. He is pretending to write a business letter but is really writing a declaration of love to Anne, which he hands her. She reads it, declares her mutual love for him, and they are married.

Persuasion, Class, and Gender

As the summary of Austen's novel suggests, *Persuasion* is full of shifting alliances and complex relationships; Austen is absorbed with how and why her characters change their minds or refuse to. Austen is aware that the quality of being firm, resolute, and decisive is considered admirable by many. In Volume 1, Chapter 10, this virtue is discussed in a conversation between Louisa Musgrove and Captain Wentworth, which Anne Elliot overhears. These three are part of a group that has undertaken a long walk to their cousin's home. While some want to turn back, Louisa insists on completing the journey. She is bragging to Captain Wentworth about her decisiveness:

> "What!—would I be turned back from doing a thing that I had determined to do, and that I knew to be right, by the airs and interference of [someone else]? . . . No,—I have no idea of being so easily persuaded."

Wentworth responds that, indeed, "the character of decision and firmness" is crucial to happiness:

> "Let those who would be happy be firm.—Here is a nut," said
> he, catching one down from an upper bough. "To exemplify,—a
> beautiful glossy nut, which, blessed with original strength, has
> outlived all the storms of autumn. . . . This nut," he continued
> with playful solemnity,—"while so many of its brethren have
> fallen and been trodden under foot, is still in possession of
> all the happiness that a hazel-nut can be supposed capable
> of." Then, returning to his former earnest tone: "My first
> wish for all, whom I am interested in, is that they should be
> firm."

Louisa responds to Wentworth with silence, and Anne Elliot seems to take the moral of his little speech quite seriously: A person who wants to lead a happy life should be firm as a nut, and not fall from that firm position and be walked over by others. In short, *resist persuasion.*

Ethos, Pathos, Logos

What is Austen trying to tell us about persuasion through this speech? At the very least, she would have us ask questions about Wentworth's motives and about Louisa's and Anne's responses:

- Is Wentworth trying to impress Louisa?
- To praise her?
- To mock her? (He delivers his speech about the nut with "playful solemnity," which may mean that he is not taking himself or his subject seriously.)
- Is he really addressing Anne, whom he perhaps knows to be hiding behind a hedgerow?
- Whether or not he is addressing Anne, is he remembering that Anne had refused him seven years ago as a result of the persuasion of Lady Russell?

- Anne concludes that he has spoken "with such serious warmth," but can we trust her evaluation of his sincerity and emotion? (She has been making lots of guesses about what he is thinking and feeling up to this point.)
- Louisa responds with silence—what does this mean?
   —That he has left her speechless with admiration?
   —Confused and uncertain about the analogy to the nut?
   —Encouraged by his affection for her?

These are the sorts of questions that should alert us to the difficulties of interpreting and understanding social conversation. Without particular reference to Wentworth, Louisa, and Anne, this scene prompts us to ask some more general questions about how we are persuaded to interpret what others say and write.

The* Ethos *of Sincerity.   How can we tell whether a speaker or writer is being serious or sincere? In February 1996, *Chicago Tribune* columnist Mike Royko wrote a column that he said was intended to mock Republican presidential candidate Pat Buchanan. In the column, Royko voiced some derogatory views of Mexicans, views that he associated with Buchanan. Hundreds of members of the Mexican community in Chicago demonstrated against Royko outside the *Tribune* building, claiming that his remarks went beyond humor and satire and were, in fact, racial insult. Statements from both sides of this controversy have done little to resolve the issue of whether Royko's *ethos* in this column exhibited goodwill toward the Mexican community through condemning Buchanan or ill will toward the Mexican community by expressing views that many Mexicans and others think should not have been written, even as satire.

Specific to Austen's *Persuasion*, we can ask whether Wentworth's speech—especially his core proposition, "Let those who would be happy be firm"—illustrates the *ethos* of practical wisdom or common sense, moral virtue, and goodwill. Certainly, this character is a man who is worldly and experienced, well beyond the confines of the neighborhoods in which Anne and Louisa live, and therefore likely to be considered more qualified to pronounce what's best for the human condition.

Certainly, Wentworth's career as a military man suggests that he has extensive experience with *firmness:* Military life is based on absolute discipline, which becomes especially crucial in battle, when life and death are at stake.

The* Pathos *of Silence.   However, Wentworth is not a man with any special knowledge of whether hazelnuts are happy or not or even whether *firm* people are happier than those who change their minds. If his supposed wisdom about firmness is persuasive, it may have more to do with the susceptibility of his audience to this viewpoint than with the authority of the evidence that he offers. The response to Wentworth here is silence on the parts of both Louisa and Anne. With *pathos* in mind, then, we might ask a general question about the function of silence, both here and as it functions more generally in conversations between women and men:

> Is silence following a personal remark an indicator of agreement? disagreement? respect? indifference? fear?

It is likely that silence says something about the emotional state, or *pathos,* of the audience. And as Deborah Tannen suggests, men can exert power over women by talking more, especially in public situations, to the point that some women may feel unqualified to speak up and therefore remain silent, rather than respond.

The pathetic appeal of Wentworth's speech seems obvious, on one level: Louisa Musgrove has been flirting with Wentworth prior to this scene in a sort of rivalry with her sister Henrietta for his affections. As the scene begins, Louisa is bragging about her own firmness: No one can persuade her to do something she doesn't want to do, Louisa insists. When Wentworth then delivers his speech in praise of firmness, he seems to be flattering Louisa. He concludes; she is silent. Given that we tend to approve of statements by others that agree with our own, Louisa's silence here might be understood as a sign of approval and affection. Her silence functions then—as it sometimes does in couples—to suggest their intimacy with one another.

By not responding, Louisa gives Wentworth the final word on this subject, and in that way, she also behaves like a student would with a teacher (Wentworth's little lecture on the nut seems very teacherlike) or like a less powerful individual would with someone more powerful. That is, her silence also functions as a kind of deference, suggesting that his opinion is beyond any improvement, criticism, or elaboration. In this connection, Louisa's silence is a result of their social class and respective genders. Recall Austen's famous opening statement from her novel *Pride and Prejudice,* cited in Chapter 2: "It is a truth universally acknowledged, that a single man in possession of a good fortune, must be in want of a wife." Austen goes on to say that this is a truth "well fixed" in all the families of an English country neighborhood. Certainly, *Persuasion,* like all of Austen's novels, features the importance of marrying well in the minds of its characters; everyone is constantly occupied with the question of who might want to marry whom. Captain Wentworth himself had declared, prior to his speech on firmness, that "it was now his object to marry" and tells his sister that he is not necessarily very particular: "Any body between fifteen and thirty may have me for asking. A little beauty, and a few smiles, and a few compliments to the navy, and I am a lost man." Above all, he wants (he says) "a strong mind, with sweetness of manner."

This is very much a scene, then, in which Wentworth and Louisa are conforming to the requirements of local society and of their respective positions as an eligible bachelor and an unmarried woman. Unmarried women typically outnumbered eligible men in Austen's society, so the luxury of choice fell to the men. To the extent that she would like to be chosen, then, a woman in Austen's world must seem to be agreeable to a man's opinions. A general point about both *ethos* and *pathos* that this scene illustrates is: "The less power one has, the more compelled one is to be agreeable." Being agreeable can often mean being silent.

The Logos *of Happy Nuts.* Let us not forget Anne Elliot, who is hiding and listening to Wentworth and evaluates his speech as warm, serious, and interesting. She knows that Wentworth wants a wife and has been hoping that—despite her earlier rejection of him—she is not altogether out of the running. Further, the *logos* of this speech is bound to have a particularly strong effect on Anne because it is so connected with how she perceives her own experience. The enthymeme that frames Wentworth's speech—"If you would be happy, you should be firm"—could likely activate the following sort of syllogistic reasoning in Anne:

> People who are not firm are unhappy.
>
> I was not firm in my acceptance of Wentworth seven years ago.
>
> Therefore, I am not happy.

In Wentworth's story of the hazelnut, another syllogism is at work, one perhaps more farfetched than any Anne or Louisa might construct based upon their personal experiences in life and love. It goes something like this:

> Firmness coincides with happiness in both the human and natural worlds.
>
> This nut has remained firm.
>
> The nut has led a long, undamaged (happy) life.

Without explicitly stating the major premise of this syllogism, Wentworth delivers the idea as an enthymeme, leaving Louisa (or us readers) to perceive the more general proposition connecting the human world of happy firmness with the natural world.

The idea of comparing oneself to a happy hazelnut seems comical, even at this time in intellectual history, when contemporaries of Jane Austen such as Samuel Coleridge and William Wordsworth were advancing the influential view that we should look for analogies to human life in the objects of nature, in rocks and stones and trees and nuts. Through his tone of voice, Wentworth seems to admit that he is not altogether serious, but the response by Anne suggests that when an audience is deeply susceptible to persuasion on two counts—*ethos* and *pathos*—the quality of the *logos* may be less crucial.

"Approving What We Like"

Throughout *Persuasion,* Austen points out that *persuasion is something we do to ourselves,* an internal process that is going on constantly as we listen to and evaluate the discourse of others with reference to our own backgrounds, needs, and desires. As Austen says very early in the novel, "How quick come the reasons for approving what we like." With this, she stresses that we can easily invent good reasons to support opinions and decisions that we favor but that when something is proposed that we dislike, our response will be that there is no good reason for doing such a thing.

Apart from the incidents in Austen's novel, everyday examples of biased self-persuasion are common. Suppose Matt doesn't like carrots. After eating them with dinner on Tuesday, he is served them again on Friday, whereupon he says, "I had carrots already this week. The most important feature of a healthy diet is variety, not the same vegetable day in and day out." His sister Jessica loves carrots and responds to Matt's complaint by saying, "You can't eat too many carrots. They're loaded with beta carotene, and as all the current studies show, that's what guards against disease."

On the one hand, both Matt and Jessica are presenting logical arguments; on the other hand, it is evident that even the most formal presentation of logical proof can reflect deep personal bias. Sir Walter's expressed dislike of sailors is an instance of this. In Volume 1, Chapter 3, when he is considering renting his estate to Admiral Croft, Sir Walter notes that the life and profession of a sailor is, in general, offensive to him and proceeds to give his reasons:

> "I have two strong grounds of objection to it. First, as being the means of bringing persons of obscure birth into undue distinction, and raising men to honours which their fathers and grandfathers never dreamt of; and secondly, as it cuts up a man's youth and vigour most horribly; a sailor grows old sooner than any other man; I have observed it all my life."

Sir Walter's logic here is based directly on the main feature of his character: vanity. As Austen tells us, "Vanity was the beginning and the end of Sir Walter Elliot's character; vanity of person and of situation." His vanity is based on an obsession with physical beauty and with social status and determines an internal logic in which two major premises are part of Sir Walter's thinking again and again:

Noble social rank is the measure of human worth.

Good looks are the measure of human worth.

Anne Elliot's opinion of sailors is decidedly unlike her father's:

> "The navy, I think, who have done so much for us, have at least
> an equal claim with any other set of men, for all the comforts and
> all the privileges which any home can give. Sailors work hard
> enough for their comforts, we must all allow."

The major premise that seems to govern Anne's thinking, in this case
and so many others, may be expressed as "Human worth can be measured in a *number* of ways." Anne Elliot stands apart from the characters
who all too readily find good reasons for advancing their likes and dislikes. Further, Anne Elliot is one of the few characters who understands
that whatever people say is true or false, good or bad, important or
unimportant is always relative to their own personal and social situations. And it is her tendency to be open minded, in sharp contrast to the
stubborn firmness of both her father and her older sister, that lowers
Anne in their estimate. They do not see her as one whose opinion has
any worth. In Volume 1, Chapter 1, we are told that she "was nobody
with either father or sister: her word had no weight; her convenience
was always to give way."

In short, Anne does not possess the firmness of the hazelnut, which
in Sir Walter is simply hard-headed stubbornness. In the realm of persuasion, we might think of someone like Anne as a generous person
who will listen well to others and try to adapt her thinking to the social
situation she finds herself in. She has no stake in forcing her opinion on
the world, but unfortunately, this lack of what we might call *assertive-
ness* results in her usual fate, which is, as we learn in Volume 1, Chapter
2 of *Persuasion*, "having something very opposite from her inclination
fixed on." Anne doesn't tend to get what she wants.

Speech Acts and Desire

For Jane Austen, one of the perils of social discourse is the tendency
for people to worry more about what *others* need and think than about
what they *themselves* need or think—or worse, to fix on what others
think of *them* more so than on what they think of *others*. Such people
can find themselves going along more than they should as well as inter-

preting the intentions of others inaccurately. This is where *speech act theory* comes in. One frequent behavior of the characters in Austen's novels is their guessing what other people mean or intend without having conclusive evidence. The central illustration of this phenomenon is the relationship between Anne and Wentworth: Even though she had rejected him seven years ago, Anne still harbors affection for Wentworth and is desperate to understand how he feels about her. But at the same time that she is wondering "how were his sentiments to be read," she is hating herself for caring, and as her emotions shift from forced indifference (an attitude of "Who cares what he thinks?") to heightened desire ("He's wonderful, and I wish I'd never said no to him"), Anne's mental process of self-persuasion changes accordingly. When Wentworth first arrives on the scene, Anne interprets his every word and action as "cold politeness" and "ceremonious grace," determined to quit hoping that their former romance might be rekindled.

Her conclusions are very different in Volume 1, Chapter 10. Just after Anne has overheard Wentworth's speech on the hazelnut, there is a small discussion among their now-tired walking party about who shall ride home with Admiral and Mrs. Croft. (There is room enough for only one.) Anne observes Wentworth say something (which she cannot hear) to the Admiral's wife (Wentworth's sister), and the next thing she knows, the Crofts are insisting that *she* ride with them. She has no idea what Wentworth has said or if it even concerned her; yet she draws a rich series of conclusions about his feelings and intentions:

> Yes,—he had done it. She was in the carriage, and felt that he had placed her there, that his will and his hands had done it, that she owed it to his perception of her fatigue, and his resolution to give her rest. She was very much affected by the view of his disposition towards her which all these things made apparent. This little circumstance seemed the completion of all that had gone before. She understood him. He could not forgive her,—but he could not be unfeeling. Though condemning her for the past, and considering it with high and unjust resentment, though perfectly careless of her, and though becoming attached to another, still he could not see her suffer, without the desire of giving her relief. It was a remainder of former sentiment; it was

an impulse of pure, though unacknowledged friendship; it was a proof of his own warm and amiable heart, which she could not contemplate without emotions so compounded of pleasure and pain that she knew not which prevailed.

Anne persuaded herself that Wentworth intended to communicate sympathy, friendship, forgiveness, and some residual love, but she never heard him speak. The speech act itself—and its illocutionary/perlocutionary force—are all constructed by her without any definite or concrete evidence.

This scene, and our emphasis to this point on how an individual's biases and needs figure into the logic of self-persuasion, support an important fact about persuasion in general: *Persuasion is a consequence of desire.* Sir Walter Elliot desires a world of people that validate his own sense of himself, and this accounts for how he persuades himself about what to approve and disapprove. Anne Elliot desires Wentworth and gives his every word and action meaning in accordance with that desire. Kenneth Burke has proposed that whenever we perceive a speech act as meaningful, it is because that act has both aroused and fulfilled a certain desire in us. As explained in Chapters 1 and 2 of this book, Burke also says that people will label the dramatic elements of an act (that is, the Act-Agent-Scene-Agency-Purpose) in different ways; this dramatism is especially striking in the concluding scenes of *Persuasion*.

Scope, Circumference, and Love

In Volume 2, Chapter 11, at a gathering in a hotel room in Bath, Wentworth's friend Captain Harville engages Anne in a discussion about which sex is more devoted to an absent lover, men or women. Harville argues that men are more "constant" than women:

> "I will not allow it to be more man's nature than woman's to be inconstant and forget those they do love, or have loved. I believe the reverse. I believe in a true analogy between our bodily frames and our mental; and that as our bodies are the strongest, so are our feelings; capable of bearing most rough usage, and riding out the heaviest weather."

By resorting to analogy, Harville constructs an enthymeme: "If men's bodies are stronger and more durable than women's, then so are our feelings." Anne counters that men forget their lovers sooner than women:

> "You have difficulties, and privations, and dangers enough to struggle with. You are always labouring and toiling, exposed to every risk and hardship. Your home, country, friends, all quitted. Neither time, nor health, nor life, to be called your own. It would be too hard indeed . . . if woman's feelings were to be added to all this."

Women, she argues, are more likely to hold onto tender feelings because they are not occupied with all the occupations and hardships of male life; instead, women "live at home, quiet, confined, and our feelings prey upon us." For men to maintain devotion to a distant or absent lover in the midst of all their other public responsibilities would be "too hard indeed."

The debate between Anne and Harville continues, with Harville finally wondering what sort of proof it will take for one side or the other to win. Anne denies that any conclusive proof is possible:

> "It is a difference of opinion which does not admit of proof. We each begin probably with a little bias towards our own sex, and upon that bias build every circumstance in favour of it which has occurred within our own circle; many of which circumstances (perhaps those very cases which strike us the most) may be precisely such as cannot be brought forward without betraying a confidence, or in some respect saying what should not be said."

With this speech, Anne summarizes the overall theory of persuasion that operates in Austen's novel: that even among the most well-intentioned and friendly debaters, *persuasion depends upon the sharing of some relevant background and bias,* and additionally—as we learn from earlier passages—*a common desire.*

In Burkean terms, Anne and Harville do not share the same scope and circumference (terms introduced in Chapter 2). As Anne suggests, in a case like this, we each have "our own circle," and as Burke would say, to the extent that those circles share a *margin of overlap,* there is the possibility that we can share a point of view. In this case, however, there is a situation within the circle that Anne and Harville share that could be used to help prove whether men or women are the more constant, and that is the relationship between Anne and Wentworth. After seven years, does Wentworth still love her or she him? This question is, of course, what Anne has in mind when she worries about saying "what should not be said," presuming that their feelings for one another must remain private and confidential.

What is remarkable about the debate between Anne and Harville is that in the act of denying the possibility of persuasion, Anne is actually successful in persuading Wentworth to declare his love for her! All the time she and Harville are speaking, Wentworth is sitting at a desk in the room, pretending to write a business letter. Actually, he is writing a letter to Anne, which he hands to her quickly and then leaves. The letter shows that Wentworth has been deeply moved by what he has overheard Anne say:

> "I can listen no longer in silence. . . . Dare not say that man forgets sooner than woman, that his love has an earlier death. I have loved none but you. Unjust I may have been, weak and resentful I have been, but never inconstant."

Anne reads Wentworth's letter, finds him in the neighborhood, and begins a conversation in which they clarify for each other all they have been thinking and feeling in recent months. They marry and by the novel's end, look forward to a happy life together.

What accounts for the strange fact that even though Anne is not speaking directly to Wentworth or specifically about her love for him, she succeeds in persuading him to do what she has wanted all along—to declare his love for her? In other words, what element of persuasion does Austen want us to associate with this climactic moment in the novel? At the risk of sounding clichéd, I propose that the answer is *love.*

To understand how love and persuasion might work together, consider Plato's *Phaedrus,* discussed in earlier chapters. This is a dialogue on the nature of love that becomes a dialogue on the nature of ideal persuasion. In it, Socrates explains that persuasion can occur most beneficially and effectively between lovers because each desires to know and possess the soul of the other; that is, they are already emotionally inclined to become closer. Kenneth Burke reinforces this idea in his *A Rhetoric of Motives* by noting that persuasion is always a kind of courtship between different kinds of people. Burke adds that successful persuasion will always be to some degree mysterious, involving a certain measure of feeling that is not reducible to concrete particulars. With Socrates and Burke in mind, we might conclude that persuasion becomes more possible and works to the best interests of those concerned when differences of bias and experience are overcome by feelings of desire and love. The relationship between persuasion and love is taken up in Spike Lee's *Do the Right Thing*, in which the voice of Mister Senor Love Daddy, a disc jockey broadcasting on WELOVE radio, resonates through a New York neighborhood, a neighborhood in which the Burkean margin of overlap, which makes both love and persuasion possible, disappears.

Spike Lee's
Do the Right Thing

It is 1989, a scorching summer day in the Bedford-Stuyvescent area of Brooklyn. Sal's Famous Pizzeria is a landmark in the neighborhood, run by the owner, Sal, and his two sons, Pino and Vito. These Italian Americans and their restaurant seem out of place in this largely black neighborhood, as does the convenience store across the street, operated by a Korean couple. But Sal seems to get along fine with the locals and is proud of maintaining—as he puts it—a "respectable business." Mookie, a young black man who lives in the neighborhood, delivers pizzas for Sal.

The action of *Do the Right Thing* takes place over one 24-hour period, from the arrival of Sal and sons at the pizzeria at about 8 A.M. to a final conversation between Sal and Mookie in front of the now-destroyed pizzeria at about the same time the next morning. With the temperature rising to over 100 degrees in the course of the day, everyone is trying to cope with the heat. The social atmosphere begins to heat up with a confrontation between Sal and one of the more activist neighborhood figures who's called Buggin Out. Preparing to sit down to a slice of pizza at Sal's, Buggin' Out pays particular attention to the Wall of Fame, which features photos of Italian American celebrities such as Frank Sinatra and Al Pacino. When Buggin' Out protests that no black people are represented, Sal—whose friendliness to others in the neighborhood doesn't seem to extend to Buggin' Out—approaches him with a baseball bat, angrily maintaining that he has the right to decorate his restaurant his way. The confrontation ends without physical violence but with Buggin' Out pledging to boycott Sal's.

Another prominent figure in the neighborhood is Radio Raheem, a young black man who carries a large, loud boom box through the streets. When he enters Sal's that afternoon, boom box blasting, Raheem and Sal have a shouting match, in which Raheem tries to order some pizza and Sal orders him to turn off the music. Raheem finally complies, but angrily.

Heat and tense encounters aside, Sal is feeling pretty good about the day by the time he closes up the restaurant. Counting the day's receipts, he speaks with appreciation for the people who love his pizza. Deciding to let in a few after-hours diners, Sal unwittingly opens the door to Buggin' Out and Radio Raheem; Buggin' Out is still angry about the Wall of Fame, and when he shows up to protest further, Raheem is with him, music turned up full. Sal, furious about the noise, destroys Raheem's boom box with a baseball bat, and Raheem, himself enraged, pulls Sal to the ground and seems intent on choking him. The police arrive and choke Raheem to death in the attempt to restrain him. Once the police leave, the neighborhood crowd—now an angry mob—turns on Sal and his sons. Mookie bashes the window of the pizzeria and the mob rushes in, tearing the place apart and finally setting it on fire. The next morning, Sal looks over the rubble of his business, Mookie arrives to demand his salary, and the neighborhood begins another day.

Persuasion, Race, and Identification

One of the points made thus far in this book has been that *persuasion can only take place within a community*—that is, among people who already see themselves as sharing certain premises, beliefs, goals, needs, desires, histories, some margin of overlap. There must be some basis for those involved to care about the welfare of one another; in other words, they must view their interaction in terms of mutual goodwill, as a kind of love, if persuasion is to be possible. At the same time, it is true that this process involves some measure of *self-love*. We have seen that in *Persuasion*, Sir Walter evaluates what others say and do and decides whether to agree or disagree with them, based upon an idealized sense of his own nobility and physical beauty. When Sir Walter decides to rent his estate to Admiral Croft, despite Sir Walter's general disdain for navy men, he has persuaded himself to do so by identifying Admiral Croft with his own interests:

> "I have let my house to Admiral Croft," would sound extremely well; very much better than to any mere *Mr.* _____ ; a *Mr.* (save, perhaps, some half dozen in the nation) always needs a note of explanation. An admiral speaks his own consequence, and, at the same time, can never make a baronet look small.

Sir Walter concludes that letting his property to someone with a distinctive title would reinforce his own dignity without at all minimizing his status as nobility. So while we might say that Sir Walter's self-love is operating here, the process is more precisely called *identification*. In *Attitudes toward History* (1959), Kenneth Burke conducts an extensive discussion of how identification works in persuasion, defining it in a way that recalls Sir Walter's decision here:

> A is not identical with his colleague, B. But insofar as their interests are joined, A is *identified* with B. Or he may *identify himself* with B even when their interests are not joined, if he assumes that they are, or is persuaded to believe so.

Louisa Musgrove and Anne Elliot both seem persuaded by the rightness of Wentworth's speech on the importance of a firm mind, largely because each identifies herself with what he says, for different reasons. Louisa does so because Wentworth's speech seems to echo the sentiments she has just expressed; Anne does so because he seems to be speaking about her in particular, about her lack of firmness in loving him. In both cases, there is an element of self-interest as identification that helps make persuasion likely.

In *Do the Right Thing*, after an angry mob of black community members destroys Sal's Famous Pizzeria, they turn to the Korean owner of the store across the street, looking to destroy his place, as well. Swinging a broom as his only defense, the Korean screams, "Me no white. Me no white. Me black. Me black. Me black." The mob's anger turns to laughter, and they decide to leave him alone, because, as Spike Lee notes in the script, they "feel for him." Here, we see the meeting of *ethos*, the character of the speaker, and *pathos*, the emotions aroused in the audience, in an act of identification. The Korean store owner is insisting, "I identify with you and your interests, not them and theirs." As Aristotle observes, persuasion often rests on the fact that "all of us must be more or less fond of ourselves" and are thus persuaded to take pleasure in our own resemblance. The Korean man is able to persuade the mob to leave him alone because they recognize that both Asians and blacks resemble each other as victims of the same bigotry. Further, Lee's note that they "feel for him" takes us back to the recognition that love is an element of persuasion.

As a walking symbol of the conflict between love and hate, Radio Raheem wears gold rings on each hand: The rings on his right hand spell *L-O-V-E*, and the rings on his left hand spell *H-A-T-E*. At one point, he presents for Mookie a fight between his right and left hands, between love and hate. Lee has said that this scene is his tribute to one of his favorite films, *The Night of the Hunter*, in which the main character is a psychopathic killer who has *LOVE* and *HATE* written on the fingers of either hand. Further, however, it is Lee's recognition that love and hate are the two essential emotional states that make nonviolent persuasion either possible or impossible.

The* Logos *of Hate.   If we can call *hate* the absence of all identification and *love* the presence of some identification, we begin to understand how impossible persuasion becomes when the parties involved see each other as completely alien. In the script for *Do the Right Thing*, Lee illustrates this problem in a series of speeches, to be shot in closeup, in which a representative of each different ethnic group in the Bedford-Stuyvescent neighborhood shouts hate epithets at the camera, targeting some other ethnic group. Mookie, the black pizza delivery man who works for Sal, insults Italians:

Mookie: Dago, wop, garlic-breath, guinea, pizza-slinging, spaghetti-bending, Vic Damone, Perry Como, Luciano Pavarotti, Sole Mio, nonsinging motherfucker.

Sal's son Pino, who maintains an "Italians are best" attitude, insults blacks viciously:

Pino: You gold-teeth, gold-chain-wearing, fried-chicken-and-biscuit-eatin', monkey, ape, baboon, big thigh, fast-running, three-hundred-sixty-degree-basketball-dunking spade Moulan Yan.

Stevie, a young Puerto Rican, insults the Asians represented by the Korean store clerk:

Stevie: You slant-eyed, me-no-speak-American, own every fruit and vegetable stand in New York, Reverend Moon, Summer Olympics '88, Korean Kick-boxing bastard.

Officer Long, one of the cops on the beat who is responsible for the death of Radio Raheem, insults Puerto Ricans:

Officer Long: Goya bean-eating, fifteen in a car, thirty in an apartment, pointed shoes, red-wearing, Menudo, meda-meda Puerto Rican cocksucker.

The Korean clerk, who eventually shouts "Me no white. Me black," insults Jews:

Korean Clerk: It's cheap, I got a good price for you, Mayor Koch, "How I'm doing," chocolate-egg-cream-drinking, bagel and lox, B'nai B'rith asshole.

In every case, cultural stereotypes constitute the *logos* of hate. Although no character speaks such epithets directly to another, Lee is pointing out that this is the mental dictionary these people use to identify one another. Perhaps we each carry an internal stock of epithets like this. Certainly, Aristotle suggests as much when he points out (as noted in Chapter 1) that people who are young are typically thought to be impulsive and those who are elderly, cynical. With such observations, he is cataloguing the cultural stereotypes of his time. Moreover, he is suggesting that it would be very difficult for an elderly person to persuade a youth, because youth and age are so incompatible and because we tend to identify with those we have defined as our own kind.

The Absence of Overlap.   The individuals shouting hate epithets in *Do the Right Thing* are refusing to acknowledge any margin of overlap between themselves and the groups they attack. That this overlap is possible is indicated when the blacks finally identify with the Korean during the final moments of the film. And in an earlier instance, just previous to the montage of racial slurs, Mookie tries to convince Pino that Pino *does* identify to some extent with black people. He points out that Pino's favorite sports star is Magic Johnson, his favorite movie star is Eddie Murphy, and his favorite rock star is Prince. Confronted with these potentially persuasive premises, Pino still refuses the conclusion that his "favorite people" are black. Instead, he insists that these celebrities are "not really black." In face of the logic of Mookie's syllogism, Pino substitutes his own:

Mookie's Syllogism

Magic Johnson, Eddie Murphy, and Prince are black.

These are three of Pino's "favorite people."

Pino's "favorite people" are black.

Pino's Syllogism

Blacks are "gold-teeth, gold-chain-wearing, . . ." etc.

Johnson, Murphy, and Prince do not fit this description.

Johnson, Murphy, and Prince are not black.

For persuasion to be possible, there must be some overlap between the way two parties define the central term of the argument. For Mookie and Pino, the term *black* must have a circumference for both that includes both Pino's favorite celebrities and people like Mookie. In that case, if Pino identifies with and loves Eddie Murphy, he might also identify with and love Mookie.

Fighting for the Right Thing. The scene that precipitates the terrible destructive violence that ends *Do the Right Thing* contains many of the elements of persuasion we have discussed to this point. It begins with Buggin' Out's complaint about Sal's Wall of Fame, which is dedicated exclusively to famous Italian Americans:

> **Buggin' Out:** Sal, how come you ain't got no brothers up on the wall here?
>
> **Sal:** You want brothers up on the Wall of Fame, you open up your own business, then you can do what you wanna do. My pizzeria, Italian Americans up on the wall.
>
> **Vito:** Take it easy, Pop.
>
> **Sal:** Don't start on me today.
>
> **Buggin' Out:** Sal, that might be fine, you own this, but rarely do I see any *Italian* Americans eating in here. All I've ever seen is black folks. So since we spend *much* money here, we do have some say.
>
> **Sal:** You a troublemaker?
>
> **Pino:** You making trouble.
>
> **Buggin' Out:** Put some brothers up on this Wall of Fame. We want Malcolm X, Angela Davis, Michael Jordan tomorrow. (Sal comes from behind the counter with his Louisville Slugger Mickey Mantle model baseball bat. Vito is by his side, but Mookie intercepts them and takes Buggin' Out outside.)
>
> **Sal:** Don't come back, either.
>
> **Buggin' Out:** Boycott Sal's. Boycott Sal's.

This scene is basically a matter of dueling enthymemes: Sal's "[Since this is] My pizzeria, [I can put] Italian Americans up on the wall" versus Buggin' Out's "Since we spend *much* money here, we do have some say." Here are the syllogisms at work:

Sal's Syllogism

The owner of a business controls all aspects of that business.

I own this pizzeria.

I control what pictures go on the wall.

Buggin' Out's Syllogism

Those who contribute to the success of a business should have a voice in business decisions.

We contribute a lot of money to Sal's business.

Our people should say who is represented on the wall.

Since Sal and Buggin' Out share no premises, it is unlikely that the *logos* of this exchange, its enthymemes, will be effective.

Further, Buggin' Out has asked that Sal's Famous Pizzeria show that it identifies with its customers, and Sal has refused. This sort of refusal is often written on restaurant menus or business signs; for instance, a number of expensive restaurants enforce a dress code for their customers, with posted statements such as "We reserve the right to refuse service to anyone not properly attired." Such signs imply "I won't identify you as a customer or identify with your needs or desires unless your physical appearance is suitable." There is no allowance for the possibility of communication, much less persuasion, when identification is denied.

Sal's response, grabbing a baseball bat and approaching Buggin' Out, clearly signals his interpretation of Buggin' Out's speech act not as a suggestion, an opinion, or an opening for discussion; rather, he sees it as a serious threat, prompting self-defense. Of course, Buggin' Out's behavior is also confrontational; there is no indication that his intention is anything but hostile, and he, too, is asserting the impossibility of identification.

Sal and Buggin' Out are at odds, as Lee's title emphasizes, about what constitutes *the right thing*. Persuasion is always an effort to get someone to *do* the right thing, to act as the persuader thinks best, but as Spike Lee illustrates through this film, the definition of *the right thing* is always changeable. In this scene, both Buggin' Out and Sal think they are doing the right thing, but the destruction that results may suggest that neither of them is right. In sum, *none* of us can claim to know absolutely what the right thing is. In the film, Lee features consistent references to both Martin Luther King, Jr., and Malcolm X, two black leaders whose speeches attempted to do the right thing about race relations. Through excerpts from their speeches, Lee reminds us that King consistently advocated nonviolence and that Malcolm X at times asserted that violent protest was the answer to racial inequity. Beliefs about the right thing can differ even among those with a considerable margin of overlap, those whose community and goals are similar.

Good Reasons. Problems of identification, irreconcilable enthymemes, confrontational speech acts, and sharply contrasting versions of the right thing are especially difficult in cases of political protest because often one side "speaks a different language" from the other and they cannot engage in a dialogue because there is little overlap between their modes of expression. Wayne Booth highlighted this problem in his book *Modern Dogma and the Rhetoric of Assent* (1974), which noted that during the late 1960s and early 1970s—when the Vietnam War was the focus of protest on college campuses throughout the United States—protesters often did not express themselves by giving what those in power recognized as good reasons. Booth's point might be illustrated by a book written by one of the protesters, with a title that is similar to that of Spike Lee's film. Jerry Rubin's *Do It!* (1970) is written as a series of accusations, declarations, and slogans like the following. Here, Rubin answers his Aunt Sadie's objection to his long hair:

> Aunt Sadie, long hair is a commie plot! Long hair gets people uptight—more uptight than ideology, cause long hair is communication. We are a new minority group, a nationwide community of longhairs, a new identity, new loyalties. We longhairs recognize each other as brothers in the street.
>
> Young kids identify short hair with authority, discipline, unhappiness, boredom, rigidity, hatred of life—and long hair with letting go, letting your hair down, being free, being open. (p. 93)

Here, Rubin, like Spike Lee, proposes that identification—a foundation for persuasion and political solidarity—is based on physical appearance, rather than the validity of one's reasons or evidence. Rubin is, without realizing it, echoing some of what Aristotle noticed about how *pathos* operates. Aristotle noted that an audience will associate the physical age of a person with certain characteristics; just so, Rubin associates short hair with a certain *pathos* (thinking especially of short-haired police officers and businessmen, whom he associates with authority and rigidity).

Booth doesn't deny our widespread participation in the sorts of protest that Jerry Rubin and Spike Lee illustrate. He insists, however, that replacing *conflict* with *community,* in which we all have the right and power to engage in persuading others to do the right thing, is only possible through the use of good reasons. Booth recommends that we do not reject out of hand any statement that can pass two tests:

1. "You have no particular, concrete grounds to doubt it."

2. "You have good reason to think all [people] who understand the problem share [the] belief" (p. 40).

Subjecting Rubin's stated belief about young kids to these requirements, we should first ask, relative to test 1, whether any concrete evidence denies Rubin's assertion. That is, do young kids as a group (in 1970, when this was written) generally associate short hair with negative characteristics? Relative to test 2, we should ask whether this belief is held by a larger population that understands the sorts of social and political problems Rubin is addressing. This is the more difficult test because, as Booth admits, it involves some initial agreement about who it is that understands the problem. During the Vietnam War era, a number of different groups in this country understood the problem of the war quite differently: military officers, church leaders, Republicans, Democrats, parents of soldiers in battle, protesters, students, professors. Between and within these groups, there was much disagreement about whether the war was necessary or unnecessary, winnable or not, and so forth.

Persuasion and Power.   When two groups or individuals understand the problem in completely different ways, then what Booth calls *shared assent* is impossible. Some of Booth's critics have pointed out that in cases in which a common understanding is not possible because different sides name the problem in different ways and express themselves very differently from one another, it is often the side with the most power that will prevail. This is illustrated when Sal picks up a baseball bat and approaches Buggin' Out and later when the black community gathers its own superior power and destroys Sal's. Power can also be used nonviolently as a way to educate a group that would otherwise remain outside the sphere of good reasons and full participation in political dialogue and persuasion. English-only laws that have been passed in some states are often advocated on this basis: that people who do not speak English should be more forcibly required to do so, in order that they will have the language to (in Booth's terms) "understand the problem[s]" of civic life as the English-speaking community does and thus become more powerful themselves. Critics of such laws say they represent more powerful individuals forcing their own language and good reasons to prevail over those of the less powerful.

The fact remains, however, that persuasion requires some measure of identification, and further, when identification is not possible and the parties involved have unequal power, some form of coercion might become the alternative to persuasion. Sal attempts coercion with a baseball bat, and Buggin' Out does so by boycotting Sal's. One additional, important question, then, is whether *equality* is a necessary element of persuasion. As noted in Chapter 1, Aristotle's *Rhetoric* is a theory of persuasion that presumes equality; Aristotle derived his principles of persuasion from a study of the Greek *polis,* the political community comprised exclusively of well-born Greek men. Consequently, Aristotle's discussion of *ethos, pathos,* and *logos* does not account for the operation of persuasion between those he considered unequals—for instance, a man and a woman or a man and a slave. The Declaration of Independence, with its emphasis on equality, presumes that free speech and debate, tools of persuasion, can only be enfranchised in a scene in which everyone has equal rights. And Kenneth Burke's emphasis on identification highlights how difficult persuasion can be when the parties do not see themselves as somehow similar to one another—that is, equal in some respect.

Summary

Jane Austen's *Persuasion* further illustrates what we called in Chapter 1 the susceptibilities, or *ideologies,* that can make persuasion more or less successful. As one of Captain Wentworth's speeches illustrates, although the *ethos* of practical wisdom, moral virtue, and goodwill may be embodied in the words someone speaks, these elements do not guarantee that the speaker is sincere. Wentworth's speech also indicates that when a speaker or writer is approved of by an audience, it may be because they are inclined to agree with what he or she says; however, an audience may also express approval (sometimes through silence) because the speaker has greater social or political power or because the audience desires the approval of the speaker. (Wentworth's listeners want *him* to like *them!*) Because Wentworth's listeners are so desirous of his approval, they do not seem to notice that the *logos* of his speech—specifically, the enthymemes he constructs—is weak.

Throughout her novel, Jane Austen suggests that all persuasion is self-persuasion; that is, we *approve* of what we are already inclined to *like*. People tend to rationalize their decisions according to their personal biases. Austen's Sir Walter is a famous example of this tendency. Austen points out that desire largely determines self-persuasion. Anne Elliot sometimes interprets what Wentworth is saying and thinking according to what she *hopes* is the case, rather than what she *knows*.

For Austen, persuasion requires that the parties involved share similar backgrounds, biases, and desires. Further, she suggests that some version of love may be required for persuasion to work; if two parties approach each other without a spirit of mutual goodwill and affection, the possibilities for persuasion may be small.

Spike Lee's *Do the Right Thing* shows that persuasion requires identification and that love and hate are two emotions central to the success or failure of persuasion. To the extent that the central characters in the film hold onto hateful cultural stereotypes of people from other racial and ethnic groups, they make themselves incapable of identification and of nonviolent persuasion. Parties lacking some measure of identification with one another—what Kenneth Burke calls a *margin of overlap*—are unable to agree what the right thing is when faced with questions of right and wrong. Such hostile parties tend to construct opposing syllogisms and enthymemes.

Coming to agreement with one another is further complicated by the problem of inequality. When one party is stronger than another—in terms of racial, cultural, or economic status—what operates in the resolution of conflict may be coercion rather than persuasion. The foundations for noncoercive, nonviolent persuasion are equal rights and opportunities.

❖ *Questions to Ask Yourself*

1. The title of this chapter, "Neighborhood Persuasions," uses the word *persuasion* in at least two different senses, both of which are parts of its dictionary definition. What are they?

2. This chapter is concerned with a novel and a film in which persuasion is central and in which identification is a key element. What other novels or films might have been substituted for *Persuasion* and *Do the Right Thing*? If you are familiar with other novels by Austen or other films by Lee, consider whether they exhibit the elements of persuasion discussed here. Which television shows may fit the discussion in this chapter? Why?

3. What current national or international conflicts are based upon problems of identification? Explain your answers.

4. The sales tax in the Bedford-Stuyvescent neighborhood has just been raised 1 percent. Try creating a 500- to 750-word dialogue among Mookie, Pino, Stevie, Officer Long, and the Korean clerk about this issue, in which you attempt to discover some margin of overlap among their views.

❖ *Writing Exercise*

Is persuasion sometimes impossible? Is violent confrontation sometimes inevitable? Using relevant examples from your experience or reading, write an essay in which you address these questions, keeping in mind the elements of persuasion we have considered to this point.

❖ *Persuasive Strategies for Student Writers*

1. Find the sections or statements in your writing in which you arouse a desire on the part of your audience and the sections or statements in which you fulfill that desire. The most obvious sort of arousal sentence is "In this essay, I will show that . . ." Its fulfillment is in showing (or proving, explaining) what you promised to show. Are there other kinds of arousal-fulfillment pairs in your writing? For instance, what sort of arousal function does the title serve?

2. How would you describe a representative member of your audience? Include physical features, clothing, likes and dislikes, social and economic status, and education. Now, keeping those same factors in mind, how would that member of your audience describe you?

4

Selling in the Super Bowl

Of the eight most watched television programs of all time, seven have been Super Bowls. Super Bowl 1997 is number four, with an estimated viewing audience of 128.9 million. But Super Bowl 1996, featuring the Dallas Cowboys versus the Pittsburgh Steelers, is in the number-one position, with a viewing audience (according to NBC) of more than 138 million people. To reach this vast audience, advertisers who bought commercial time during the 1996 Super Bowl paid $2.4 million per minute, or $40,000 per second. In areas other than advertising, the Super Bowl is likewise an expensive production, featuring a high-priced corps of announcers and analysts and state-of-the-art television technologies.

Clearly, this annual event is regarded as one of the most important media opportunities to affect a large viewing audience. In this chapter, we will examine the effects that the Super Bowl telecast seeks in order to continue our general discussion of the elements of persuasion and also to gain some insight into the persuasive tactics and techniques used in staging a major cultural event—tactics and techniques that are widely employed not only in sports telecasts but generally in commercial telecasts, as well.

To begin to understand the Super Bowl in terms of persuasion, we might think of it as a long speech addressed to a large audience. While it is not an obvious piece of oratory, such as the televised State of the Union address (which we will examine in Chapter 5), the Super Bowl does employ both verbal and visual strategies to engage an audience and to encourage them to share certain points of view. The nature of those points of view will become clearer as we continue, but for now, we can say that any telecast—from the State of the Union address to the Super Bowl—embodies three basic purposes of communication. These three purposes, established centuries ago in ancient Roman textbooks, are:

1. To teach
2. To please
3. To move

All three purposes are often enacted in a single discourse. When President Clinton speaks on the State of the Union, he is, at times, explicitly seeking *to teach* the audience by delivering facts and statistics; seeking *to please* the audience through expressions of gratitude for jobs well done; and primarily seeking *to move* the audience, that is, to incline them favorably toward the policies and programs he is proposing. Similarly, when Jay Leno delivers a monologue on *The Tonight Show,* he is, in effect, teaching when he provides facts and statistics from recent news events as the entry into a joke; attempting to move the audience when he announces the guest list for the show, seeking applause that signals appreciation and support for what is to follow; and most obviously, attempting to please the audience by saying the sorts of things that provoke laughter.

These three purposes of communication—to teach, to please, and to move—can each be understood as a type of speech act, specifically, a kind of *performative.* We have considered the performative force of various speech acts in previous chapters, mainly with reference to interpersonal communication and in order to note situations in which the *illocutionary* force of the speech act (its apparent intention) does not match the *perlocutionary* force of the speech act (its effect). The mismatch between illocution and perlocution will not be our central concern in this chapter, however. Instead, we will frame this discussion primarily with reference to some of the Aristotelian and Burkean elements of persuasion we have discussed before, especially *identification.*

Teaching, pleasing, and moving all entail persuasion. When a teacher tells the class "Now I will review the facts and concepts you will need to know for the final exam," she illustrates one of the main goals of persuasive teaching: to convince the audience that the material is worth knowing. A standard line for standup comics who are not getting laughs is "These are the jokes, folks"; with this, the comedian signals his or her failure to convince the audience to feel pleased. The last of the three purposes for communication, to move, is the one most obviously connected with persuasion, and its success is measured by the audience's decisions: as voters moved by campaign speeches, as consumers moved by advertisements.

We generally don't regard entertainment events such as the Super Bowl as persuasion events, although we do recognize that television commercials are calculated to persuade. Rather, we often turn to television as an *alternative* to the world of persuasion. People commonly say that they watch TV "just to be entertained" and thus define the purpose of most programming as *to please,* rather than *to teach* or *to move.* Defining entertainment in this way, as an innocent pleasure, sets aside a significant fact: Television, and all mass market entertainment, is a commodity that we are being sold. In other words, the goal of any television program is to convince us to buy the sort of pleasure it offers. The appeal to our sense of pleasure is—like any piece of persuasion—an appeal to our values, beliefs, and desires. For this reason, the pleasure we derive from TV is never innocent; that is, it is never value neutral.

Many historians of television, looking back on the so-called golden age of the 1950s and 1960s, now recognize that the most popular programs of those years—*I Love Lucy, Father Knows Best, Leave It to Beaver,* and *The Donna Reed Show*—were all distorted representations of family life. They encouraged audiences to regard the typical American family as white, affluent, and happy, or at least without any serious or insoluble problems. To the extent that television audiences were entertained— pleased—by such portrayals, their own values concerning family life were conditioned and reinforced and their sense of what a family should be was perhaps distorted. Television continues to appeal to and affect beliefs, values, and desires, and the vastly popular Super Bowl is a significant indicator of the kinds of pleasure that the viewing public is sold.

In this chapter, we will consider first the ways in which the 1996 Super Bowl attempted to please, looking closely at the halftime show in the context of the larger telecast. We will then survey the commercials distributed throughout the telecast as the most apparent examples of attempts to move an audience. And finally, we will see that while teaching may be a less obvious function of the Super Bowl, it contributes to the positive *ethos* of the telecast and its announcers.

To Please:
The *Pathos* of the Halftime Show

In Chapter 3, we paid some attention to Aristotle's observation that "all of us must be more or less fond of ourselves" and that we take pleasure in our own resemblance. It would follow, then, that a presentation that seeks to please us will to some extent reflect our own backgrounds, desires, experiences, and beliefs. This was certainly the effort of the halftime show for the 1996 Super Bowl, which featured Diana Ross in a spectacular medley of her hit songs, capped by her departure from the field in a helicopter while singing "I Will Survive." The sheer spectacle of this presentation will concern us eventually, but for the moment, let's consider the several ways in which the halftime show attempted to get the audience to take pleasure in seeing themselves.

Nostalgia:
Remembering the Good Old Days

The show was titled "The Oscar Mayer Halftime Show" and was immediately preceded by a commercial featuring current-day children singing the Oscar Mayer Wiener song that was popular decades earlier. This selection of theme indicates that the target audience for the halftime show was, in general, baby boomers: people born between 1946 and 1964, who were old enough to have listened to and, in effect, memorized the Oscar Mayer song, as it was played repeatedly during their youth on television and radio commercials. With this reference to the past as a lead-in, we might have expected the halftime show to attempt to please a baby-boomer audience by appealing to their nostalgia. *Nostalgia* is most often understood as the desire to re-experience something that happened long ago; thus, it goes along with idealizing the past. Nostalgia is a powerful psychological force: As people age and their adult responsibilities increase in number and complexity, they yearn more and more for a time when life seemed more simple, free, innocent, and happy (regardless of whether this was actually true about the past). In the 1970s, the appearance of the television show *Happy Days,* about a 1950s family, began an era of nostalgia entertainment that still seems to be going strong. One of the most popular movies of the 1980s was *The Big Chill* (1983), which featured a group of old friends—brought together for the funeral of one of them—reminiscing about old times. Part of the nostalgia movement has been the labeling of the 1950s and 1960s as television's "golden age." In line with this perception, we have had 1990s movie remakes of popular old TV shows, such as *The Brady Bunch* (1995), *Sergeant Bilko* (1996), and *Mission Impossible* (1996), along with the great popularity of cable television stations such as Nickelodeon, which feature reruns of so-called classic TV. These trends constitute a widely practiced appeal to nostalgia.

The appeal to nostalgia is effective when it creates a psychological resemblance between the audience and the past self that they desire. At the 1996 Super Bowl, the agent of that resemblance was Diana Ross. Ross was at the height of her popularity in the 1970s, when a number of her recorded songs were big hits; their music and lyrics are familiar to many who lived during that era. At the Super Bowl, Ross performed an 11-minute medley of those hits. What follows is a summary version of the show. The appeal to nostalgia will be evident from the song titles, which should be immediately familiar to any baby-boomer readers of this book and may strike younger readers as either unfamiliar or antiquated. Nostalgia was also provoked by surrounding Ross with dancers who (as the summary notes) resemble Michael Jackson, the 1995 Super Bowl halftime star as well as a legendary performing partner with Ross; the association with Jackson is bound to provoke memories of both past Super Bowls and past performances by Ross and thus reinforce nostalgia.

Following this summary, we will focus on two other persuasive appeals, in addition to nostalgia, that are evident in the halftime show: (1) the appeal of spectacle and (2) the advertisement of love as a universal ideal.

The Halftime Show:
A Descriptive Summary

A white stage, 30 yards wide, is set up at midfield. At center stage, three staircases (one hidden from the cameras) lead up to a pedestal, where Ross appears—as if magically, amidst rising smoke—in a sparkling, bright-red dress, singing "Stop! In the Name of Love."

Male dancers ascend the staircases, each dressed in a suit and black hat reminiscent of the familiar costume of superstar singer and sometimes partner of Diana Ross, Michael Jackson. Surrounding the stage, filling the football field, are hundreds of people, arranged so that their bodies spell

Diana Ross

The pedestal Ross appears on is slowly lowered to the stage floor, where she greets the audience with "Hello World." The songs Ross performs are as follows:

- "Stop! In the Name of Love"
- "You Keep Me Hangin' On"
- "Baby Love"—Hundreds of dancers march around the pedestal holding different-colored hearts, which they flash in various patterns as the performance continues.
- "You Can't Hurry Love"—Ross ascends a staircase, flanked by "Michael Jackson" dancers, and waves to the stadium crowd behind her when she reaches the top. Puffs of smoke come from the stage.
- "Why Do Fools Fall in Love?"—Ross descends the staircase while singing. At the conclusion of this number, onfield dancers form a heart around the stage and release hundreds of red, white, and blue balloons.
- "Chain Reaction"—Ross dons the second of four different costumes just before beginning this number. Skyrockets fire from the stage, and while Ross sings, the stadium audience, visible behind the stage, holds up cards that form the word *LOVE* in yellow letters, dozens of rows tall, on a blue background.

- "Reach Out and Touch (Somebody's Hand)"—Just before beginning this number, Ross asks, "Do you believe in love?" As she sings, the camera surveys little children holding hands and singing along on the field. Onfield dancers bounce inflated world globes in the air, back and forth between one another.

- "Ain't No Mountain High Enough"—As the song begins, people of different racial/ethnic groups and ages, all smiling, march in rows around the stage; the camera features their diversity by surveying their faces. Ross changes costumes again as she begins to sing and, in the course of this number, is lifted on the pedestal higher and higher above the stage, as those below reach their hands toward her.

- "I Will Survive"—While the chorus of singers/dancers refrains "I will survive," Ross leaves to allow a helicopter to land center stage. She boards the helicopter and is lifted away. One camera stays with the copter departure, and another from the Budweiser blimp overhead gives a full view of the stadium below. Skyrockets go off all around the stadium.

The Pleasure of Alternative Realities

The three persuasive appeals of the halftime show—to nostalgia, spectacle, and love—all have one factor in common: Each plays upon the audience's desire for an *alternative reality.* People often talk about entertainment as an escape and thus associate pleasure with escaping from the often routine, dull, difficult, and sometimes even oppressive elements of everyday life. At the same time that nostalgia entertainment appeals to pleasure through identification, it also transports us away from the present moment in an act of escape. Because spectacle features the *extra*-ordinary, it illustrates for us a dimension of reality that is, once again, an alternative to the everyday. And love is an ideal that is more desired than any other but one perceived by most of us to be in very short supply; for this reason, a world full of love, which is the world Diana Ross sings about, is also an alternative reality.

Having given attention earlier to the appeal to nostalgia, we will focus next on the appeals to spectacle and love.

Spectacle.   A *spectacle* is a visual demonstration of extraordinary size, scope, and design. The alternative reality created by spectacle often consists of elements that seem magical and/or fantastic. In this case, we have Diana Ross appearing out of nowhere amidst puffs of smoke; she is a magical figure both because she seems to materialize in an almost supernatural way and because she is such a superstar. Superstars are often regarded as being far above the run of common humanity, leading charmed lives, and so on; these impressions lend a magical quality to their identities.

Complementing the magical quality of the halftime show is the featuring of *ascension:* Ross repeatedly goes up staircases and sings from the heights, and she is finally lifted away, out of sight and into the heavens. Morevoer, skyrockets shoot high into the sky. All of these features contribute to associating love, happiness, and pleasure with magically rising above the ordinary world; the featuring of ascension is also consistent with religious beliefs about death and the afterlife, involving ascension out of this world and into a heavenly paradise.

The term *fantastic,* of course, refers to phenomena that seem more associated with fantasy than reality. In this connection, the major fantasy advanced by the halftime show is the spectacle of thousands of people behaving in perfect cooperation with one another: onfield performers of all ages and races/ethnicities forming huge, complex designs and spectators from the stands acting together to spell words and pictures that span hundreds of feet. When Diana Ross says "Hello World," she stresses that the sheer size and scope of this fantastic community is one element of spectacle.

Magical technology is another element of spectacle: Diana Ross is lifted up and down on a giant mechanical pedestal, fireworks and skyrockets blaze into the sky, and a helicopter lifts her up and away. With these events, we are treated to the spectacle of machines that can create grand, superhuman effects—colossal light shows and flying superstars.

The spectacle of technology is a consistent feature of the Super Bowl telecast. The pregame activities also feature fireworks and skyrockets, along with fighter planes streaking across the sky during the singing of "The Star-Spangled Banner." And as we will see later in the discussion of persuasive teaching, the network's coverage of the game itself is full of technological wizardry, from slow-motion replays to multiple camera angles to "chalk" diagrams of the play action drawn onscreen. Add to this the high-tech effects of the commercials (also discussed later), and it seems appropriate to regard the Super Bowl as a general advertisement for technology. To the extent that we are persuaded to take pleasure in technological spectacle, we are being sold on the value of technology itself.

Love. During the halftime show, words, symbols, and images of love abound, from the lyrics of the songs to Ross's bright-red dress to the sight of little children holding hands and a diversity of people marching together in harmony. What amounts here to the spectacular advertisement of love is very common in the entertainment industry and serves as the basis of some very well-known appeals. For instance, recall the famous TV commercial from the 1970s for Coca-Cola, in which hundreds of children from around the world sing the lyric "I'd like to buy the world a Coke," suggesting that sharing Coca-Cola will help achieve worldwide harmony and love. Also, consider the now legendary recording of "We Are the World" in 1985, a song written by Quincy Jones as a plea for donations to USA for Africa, in order to provide humanitarian relief to impoverished countries; Jones gathered dozens of the biggest stars in the music and entertainment world into a recording studio for an all-night session, in which they all sang together about the importance of love and charity. The music video version of this song still plays regularly on cable TV stations such as VH-1.

Both of these spectacular appeals to love were phenomenally successful: The Coke commercial melody became a popular music standard, and "We Are the World" brought in millions in charitable donations. These instances attest to what another popular song calls "the power of love" and verify that love is universally regarded as what people most desire yet most lack. Further, as we saw in the Chapter 3 discussions of *Persuasion* and *Do the Right Thing* and in the instances just discussed, love is the emotion most associated with identification and community.

Love remains a powerful concept for these reasons and also because it is—like truth—one of those ultimate terms that everyone can define according to his or her own biases. When Diana Ross asked the halftime audience "Do you believe in love?" it should have reminded us of Dudley Field Malone exhorting the value of truth in the Scopes trial; in both cases, an abstract term was invoked in order to dissolve any differences among members of the audience. Ideally, everyone participating in the show—performers and audience alike—is persuaded to affirm their identification with one another ("Yes, we all believe in love").

Love or War?

With these observations, let us recall the persuasive purpose of entertainment, which is to evoke in us feelings of pleasure. During the halftime show, pleasure is illustrated in the form of an alternative reality: a spectacular ideal community, in which we all march and sing together in the midst of dazzling technological wonders. However, the kind of pleasure that this halftime show provokes is at odds with the kind of pleasure provoked by the game itself and leads us to wonder how a viewer can be persuaded to identify with sharply different kinds of pleasure in the course of the entire Super Bowl program. Like the halftime show, the game provides pleasure and entertainment largely through the element of *identification:* Sports fans tend to identify to some degree with one team or another. The precise nature of this identification continues to be debated by psychologists. Their central questions are as follow:

- Does watching and cheering on competitive aggression give fans a safe outlet for their own bottled-up hostility, or does sports spectating cultivate and encourage aggressive behavior among fans?

- Moreover, does identification with skilled athletes actually raise the self-esteem of those spectators who identify with the winning team? (It is clear that spectators whose favored team is winning the game display more indications of pleasure than those whose team is losing.)

Rhetorical theorists Barry Brummett and Margaret Duncan, in a scholarly article called "Theorizing without Totalizing: Specularity and Televised Sports," propose that identification with athletes and teams can become *narcissism*, in which "we see ourselves using or linked with the goods we admire" (1990, p. 237). We see this phenomenon in the little boy who wants to grow up to be like basketball star Michael Jordan and in the group of friends who play football at a local playground on weekends in amateur imitation of the professional stars they admire. As with the halftime show, pleasure through identification has some connection to the desire for an alternative reality. Brummett and Duncan cite studies that feature the importance of vicarious experience to the fans, who take pleasure in experiencing a winning team's success as their own. On a darker note, pleasure through identification may lead to fans imitating violence on the field through violence off the field. There have been repeated instances of destructive riots in the streets of a city whose team has just won a sports championship, and there is ongoing concern about whether men identifying with sports events are more liable to commit domestic violence. (Some groups have reported that domestic violence increases significantly on Super Bowl Sunday.)

The halftime show was an advertisement for love, but professional football is nothing of the kind. As movies such as *North Dallas Forty* have illustrated, football is a brutal, bruising sport, more like a battle than a game. The military quality of the game is reinforced in the opening ceremonies by the singing of "The Star-Spangled Banner," which stresses the patriotic purpose of war. In the case of the 1996 Super Bowl, this musical tribute was accompanied by the appearance overhead of F-16 fighter planes flying in unison.

Before the game began, the announcers told us that the Dallas Cowboys had been slow to enter the field from their locker room and noted that they seemed to be deliberately walking very slowly into the stadium; the announcers speculated that this was the Cowboys' way of sending a message to the Steelers that the Cowboys were in charge of this event. The Cowboys' behavior and the announcers' commentary maintained the atmosphere of combat and conflict, which continued in the main purpose of the game itself, which is, simply speaking, to knock down the opposition. Seeing the other team as the enemy is common in professional sports, so much so that a headline on the sports page of the June 5, 1996, *Chicago Sun-Times,* heralding the start of the National Basketball Association championship series between the Chicago Bulls and the Seattle Supersonics, said "Let The Hate Begin."

How Do You Spell Relief? L-O-V-E

To have Diana Ross, singing of love, appear on the scene halfway through the Super Bowl could be regarded as too drastic a change in the appeal of the entertainment to continue to evoke pleasure from the audience. Those spectators who were taking pleasure from conflict were suddenly asked to take pleasure from love. Imagine the difficulty of keeping the audience engaged and feeling entertained if this were an oration (a continuous speech), rather than a televised "speech." The speaker would spend an hour telling vivid tales of battles, encouraging the audience to share the thrill of his victories and to applaud the defeat of the enemy. Then he would begin, abruptly, to praise the glories of love and peace. Perhaps some of the audience would leave as a kind of protest and an indication that they were no longer persuaded to take pleasure in the speech. Similarly, perhaps some of the Super Bowl television audience left off viewing during the halftime show, breaking for a snack or some fresh air. But the viewing audience did not disappear, so our question is: How is it possible for viewers to continue to feel entertained when the nature of the appeal to pleasure has become, in effect, the opposite of what it was?

In order to consider the persuasive effect of the halftime show in connection with this problem, we return to Kenneth Burke. As noted in earlier chapters, Burke is concerned with the psychological processes that make persuasion possible. One of the questions he raises is how we determine when the parts of a discourse—in this case, the Super Bowl— fit appropriately together. Our sense of the appropriateness of the fit between parts has a significant effect on our evaluation of what is being presented. In order to be gratified by anything we read, see, or hear, we must perceive that it has *form;* that is, that the parts are *coherent.* We would not likely be gratified, for instance, if Bill Clinton broke into a tap dance in the middle of the State of the Union address; such an act would constitute inappropriate form, leaving us amazed and confused and unable to take seriously any of the persuasive points that the president had made. We would have a similar response, if, for instance, irrelevant statistics started to appear onscreen during the telecast of the Super Bowl—such as the weather conditions in New Zealand or the number of traffic fatalities over the Memorial Day weekend—or if one of the announcers suddenly began singing Broadway show tunes or describing in great detail what he or she ate for breakfast.

Such acts would be regarded as breaches in form if we adopt Burke's definition: "*Form* . . . is an arousing and fulfillment of desires. A work has form in so far as one part of it leads a reader [or in our case, a viewer] to anticipate another part, to be gratified by the sequence"

(*Counter-Statement,* 1968, p. 124). Two kinds of form that Burke discusses concern us here: syllogistic form and qualitative form. *Syllogistic* form is achieved when, as Burke says, "Given certain things, certain things must follow, the premises forcing the conclusion" (p. 124). Syllogistic form has been illustrated in a number of syllogisms and enthymemes in this book so far, and we have seen that when syllogistic form is effective, we are persuaded that the sequence of statements or actions is correct. Burke suggests the possibility of what we might call a *dramatic* syllogism, in which an observed sequence of events strikes us as correct or desirable—in a story, for instance, in which a crime is followed by a punishment or a good deed is followed by a reward.

The Super Bowl halftime show would seem to be, in certain ways, a violation of syllogistic form, with a celebration of war leading to a celebration of love. However, the halftime show is effective as an illustration of *qualitative* form. Qualitative form works, according to Burke, when "we are put into a state of mind which another state of mind can appropriately follow" (p. 125). Significantly, his examples of qualitative form are all instances of *contrast.* He notes, for instance, that in William Shakespeare's *Macbeth,* Macbeth's gruesome murder of King Duncan is followed by a comic scene involving a porter; the deep seriousness of one scene prepares us for the comic antics of the next. With such examples, Burke suggests that contrast serves the function of psychological relief and gratifies us because we do indeed desire that relief (perhaps without consciously realizing it). In the Super Bowl, then, a show about love gratifies our desire for relief from war.

Happy Consciousness

Another possibility that explains why we are entertained by such radically different appeals to pleasure is suggested by Herbert Marcuse, a modern philosopher who is particularly interested in how social events affect our behavior. Marcuse, along with other members of the Frankfurt School, a group of philosophers who apply Marxist principles to the study of mass culture, has proposed that we tend to look to the larger society—and its institutions, such as the entertainment industry—for our definitions of pleasure. To the extent that we regard television as an official cultural agent of entertainment, we accept whatever it presents to us as such and do not raise questions about what values the entertainment is advertising or whether the types of pleasure it is evok-ing are contradictory. In other words, as we watch TV, a kind of govern-ing syllogism like this operates:

Television is entertainment.

I am watching television.

Therefore, I am being entertained.

For Marcuse, the main goal of the larger society is to maintain in in-dividuals a *happy consciousness,* which does not consider alternatives to what is offered for consumption and buys whatever the larger society has to sell. Critics of this view say that it portrays individuals as witless dupes, without the intellectual power or freedom to resist the persuasive power of the larger society and its institutions; these critics insist that the more fully we accept that the media can manipulate us, the more they will.

Another manifestation of happy consciousness is the tendency to ac-cept without criticism unrealistic or oversimplified solutions to human problems. When television programming appeals to our desires for an alternative reality, it may also lead to some confusion of that reality with actual life problems and solutions. The desire for an alternative reality is mainly addressed by comedy and variety shows. Although the portrayal of everyday life on television is less unrealistic than it was in the days of *Father Knows Best,* many television critics worry that the typical televi-sion sitcom still solves social and personal problems too simply and effi-ciently, in less than 30 minutes. For instance, the 1996 season finale of a highly popular sitcom, *Mad About You,* featured the two characters—a married couple—in a series of angry and emotional discussions about whether they should stay together and about their frustration at not being able to conceive a child. During the final few minutes of the show, they abruptly declare their love and devotion to one another, make love, and—as we learn in the final seconds of the show—conceive a child.

The alternative to happy consciousness is *critical consciousness,* which is, basically, the ability to detect and evaluate the elements of per-suasion that are operating in the larger society. Nowhere is critical con-sciousness more important than in our response to advertising, in which the overt purpose is to affect our decisions and behaviors—or, in connection with the three purposes of persuasion we are discussing in this chapter, to move.

To Move:
Commercials and *Kairos*

President Calvin Coolidge offered a well-known definition of *advertising,* describing it as "the method by which the desire is created for better things." We have discussed the ways in which the halftime show advertises nostalgia, spectacle, and love in order to appeal to the desire for an alternative reality. The Super Bowl commercials are less interested in maintaining a state of mind among the viewers (what Marcuse calls *happy consciousness*) than in moving them to take action: to buy or consume a product.

Several methods are used to achieve the goal of moving the viewer toward the consumption or purchase of what is perceived as something better. One of these methods is the arrangement of the commercials so that they are played at times when a viewer's interest in a particular sort of product is likely to be strongest. For instance, household cleaners tend to be advertised on daytime television, when viewers tend to be those people who do household cleaning; we might conclude that an advertiser buying time for a laundry detergent commercial during *The Tonight Show* is ignoring the persuasive effect of the appropriate arrangement of commercial appeals.

The effective persuasive arrangement of commercial advertising can be considered in terms of a full day of programming, with reference to the kinds of viewers who are likely to be watching at different times and what their needs and desires might be. However, the Super Bowl provides a unique opportunity to study the arrangement of commercial advertising with reference to a social viewing event that lasts about four hours, during which the activities, needs, and desires of viewers change and during which the arrangement of commercials takes those changes into account.

By focusing on arrangement to begin this discussion of commercial advertising, we are stressing what ancient Greek rhetoricians called *kairos,* which might be translated as "timeliness." The concept of *kairos* reflects the belief that the success or failure of persuasion depends upon presenting the right thing at the right time. The importance of *kairos* is stressed by some ancient rhetoricians who have been associated with the deceptive manipulation of language. This group, known as the *sophists,* has been accused (unfairly, in many cases) of caring only about gaining advantage over the audience, not about telling the truth. But even Plato, who was an opponent of the sophists, alludes to the concept of *kairos* when he says in *Phaedrus* that an ideal speech must be "exactly attuned to every changing mood of the complicated soul." In other words, as the audience changes, so must our persuasive appeals.

In order to discuss the ways in which the arrangement of commercials during the Super Bowl takes into account the changing moods of viewers, let's consider a tally of the kinds of products advertised, divided into the two main segments of the telecast: the first half of the game and the second half.

First-Half Commercials

In the following lists, the numbers in parentheses indicate the numbers of commercials telecast in each category and for each product:

Food (11):	M&Ms (1)
	Doritos (3)
	Baked Lays Chips (1)
	Pork (2)
	Pizza Hut (2)
	McDonald's (2)
Cars/Motorcycles (8):	Plymouth (4)
	Nissan Pathfinder (1)
	Toyota 4-Runner (1)
	Yamaha (1)
	BMW (1)
Investment/Financial Products (4):	Prudential (1)
	Principal Investment Group (2)
	Visa (1)
Nonalcoholic Beverages (4):	Pepsi (4)
Alcoholic Beverages (3):	Budweiser (3)
	(The Budweiser blimp, equipped with a camera, views the game from above the stadium and appears at various points throughout the telecast.)

NBC Television (3):	NBC Sports(1)
	Friends (1)
	Gulliver's Travels (1)
	(These are 30-second spots; various briefer spots for NBC occur throughout the telecast.)
Sports Gear (2):	Nike (2)
Business/ Communication (2):	Kinko's (1) Ameritech (1)
Home Hardware (1):	Masterlock (1)
Travel (1):	British Airways (1)
Medication/Pain Relief (1):	Tylenol (1)
National Football League (1)	

Second-Half Commercials

NBC Television (8):	*Friends* (2)
	Mad About You (1)
	Dateline NBC (1)
	NBC Tuesday Night Lineup (1)
	Summer Olympics (1)
	NBC Sunday Night Lineup (1)
	Seinfeld (1)
Cars (6):	Dodge (1)
	Honda (1)
	Ford (3)
	Nissan (1)
Investment/Financial Products (6):	American National Bank (2) Prudential (1) MasterCard (2) Visa (1)
Medication/Pain Relief (4):	Pepcid AC (1)
	Advil (1)
	Tylenol (1)
	Breathe Right Nasal Strips (1)

Alcoholic Beverages (3):	Budweiser (3)
Business/	Ameritech (2)
Communication (3):	Mail Boxes, Etc. (1)
Food (3):	Subway (1)
	Wheaties (1)
	Snickers (1)
Nonalcoholic Beverages (2):	Pepsi (2)
Entertainment (2):	Primestar Satellite TV (1)
	Independence Day (1)
Car Products (1):	Slick 50 Fuel System (1)
Sports Gear (1):	Nike (1)
Home Hardware (1):	Owens Corning Insulation (1)
Travel (1):	Air Jamaica (1)

From Pizza to Pepcid AC

The arrangement of commercial spots by the advertisers and the network presumes that a certain audience psychology operates during the game. It presumes, first of all, that the audience consists mainly of adult men. Although there is some evidence that the number of women sports fans is increasing and that women may account for between 30 and 40 percent of the football viewing audience, the target audience continues to be men. Taking race into account, we should note that NFL football telecasts, including the Super Bowl, constitute the only type of top-10 programming that is a favorite across racial lines. As we will see, the arrangement of commercials also suggests that the Super Bowl is watched on television by groups of viewers who make the game a social event, rather than by individuals who watch alone.

With this audience in mind, imagine a group of perhaps six or eight people, most of them adult men, gathered together in a living room on Super Bowl Sunday, to eat and drink and watch the game. Of the 41 30-second commercial spots during the first half of the 1996 game, 18 were for food and drinks. Six of the 11 food commercials were run before the kickoff, immediately before and after the singing of the national anthem, and 4 more were arranged immediately before and after the 2-minute warning that signals the end of the first half. In other words, food advertising occurred at moments when viewers were not likely to be engrossed in the game yet or when they may have been contemplating how to fill the time during the halftime break; these were the times when they were most likely to run out and buy some burgers at Mc-Donald's or phone Pizza Hut for delivery. (One past advertiser for the Super Bowl—Domino's Pizza—reported that pizza deliveries during halftime in the city whose team is winning are extremely high.) First-half advertisements for Pepsi and Budweiser seemed less calculated to elicit immediate buying, distributed as they were throughout the 14 commercial breaks that preceded the halftime show. But of course, if every drink commercial sends someone to the refrigerator for a beverage—something viewers can do during any commercial break without missing any play action—it makes it more likely that someone will need to go out and buy more drinks at halftime.

After foods and drinks, the products most frequently advertised during the first half of the 1996 Super Bowl were automobiles. Plymouth featured 4 commercials for its new Breeze, a compact and relatively inexpensive family car that may have appealed both to male viewers with small families and to their spouses who were watching. The other automobiles advertised were decidedly more masculine in their appeal: recreational vehicles associated with off-road activities, such as hunting and fishing (Nissan Pathfinder, Toyota 4-Runner); a motorcycle featured as the vehicle for the rugged male individual on the open road (Yamaha); and a luxury car typically associated with business and professional men. The car commercials did not appear to be strategically arranged; rather, they aimed for what was more likely an ongoing interest on the part of the audience, rather than (as in the case of foods and drinks) an immediate interest.

The rest of the commercials—for financial and investment products, business equipment, sports gear, hardware (door locks), executive travel, and pain relief—allow us to construct the target consumer as a man in a management or executive position who worries about the financial future and physical safety of his family, who travels on business occasionally, who wears athletic gear for amateur weekend sports contests, and who gets a headache now and then.

During the second half of the 1996 Super Bowl, the proportion and arrangement of commercials changed significantly. The number of food and drink commercials dropped from 18 to 8; only 3 of these were for food, and 2—for Wheaties and Subway—were for products viewers might purchase the next day or the next week but not for the game. The number of commercials for Budweiser matched that of the first half, suggesting that the consumption of beer is seen as an activity that continues all through the game. The number of automobile commercials was slightly higher but, as in the first half, did not suggest any focused appeal to an immediate desire on the part of the audience. We might note, however, that automobiles have long represented alternative reality to consumers, associated as they are with getting away from mundane reality, with recreation, and with individual freedom. In this connection, the appeal to new-car desire is similar to the appeals to nostalgia, spectacle, and love discussed earlier; all are categories of alternative reality.

The top category for advertising during the second half of the game was NBC television. At this point, the network envisioned a viewer who was looking ahead to future entertainment—now that the pizza, Doritos, and beer had been consumed and the outcome of the game was perhaps more clear. In general, then, the arrangement of commercials to appeal to immediate needs and desires was less apparent during the second half than during the first, except in one category: medication/pain relief. The 4 commercials that appeared in this category pointed directly at a viewer who's had too much to eat and drink and perhaps exercised too much fan exertion while watching the game. From the beer and junk food, he has developed a headache (and needs Advil or Tylenol) or a stomach ache (and needs Pepcid AC), and it is possible that the physical distress will worsen his snoring—hence, the need for Breathe Right Nasal Strips.

Anthropomorphic Identification

To a great extent, commercial advertising in the Super Bowl exploits both *desire* and *identification,* and so it coincides with the persuasive strategies operating during the telecast of the play action as well as the halftime show. However, identification, which we have seen to be a significant element of persuasion in so many of the texts we have discussed in this book, takes a strange turn in many commercials, which feature *anthropomorphic* characters (nonhuman characters behaving like humans). Such commercials prompt us to ask, for instance, how human viewers identify with and are moved by life-size talking M&Ms, a fish that drinks Pepsi, a Tyrannosaurus Rex skeleton that eats McDonald's fries, penguins driving BMWs, beer-drinking vultures, and horses playing football (in a Budweiser commercial). In addition to these anthropomorphic characters, we are treated to other instances of the unnatural: a man whose neck stretches to the length of that of a giraffe; a parade of tiny men marching in the palm of a normal man's hand (both in a Kinko's commercial); and a field of corn that explodes into popcorn as a new car (a Plymouth) passes on the road. Certainly, featuring an alternative reality in each of these cases appeals to the desire for entertainment as escape and is consistent with other kinds of alternative-reality appeals we have discussed.

But how do we identify with this reality? One answer to this question recalls our previous discussion of technological spectacle and looks ahead to our discussion of the ways in which the Super Bowl uses sophisticated graphics and data-retrieval systems to keep us updated on the play action and the players. What the Super Bowl advertises through a number of means—anthropomorphic commercials included—is *technology*. From the impressive displays of facts and statistics during the game to the dazzling display of technological wonders in the halftime show to the commercials that employ computer-generated imaging to create giant M&Ms, the Super Bowl appeals to the audience's appreciation for special technical effects. Moroever, this approach illustrates a clear working assumption on the part of the network and its advertisers that technical effects contribute to the positive state of mind that is necessary to persuasive teaching, pleasing, and moving.

Many who have studied the tremendous growth of technology and the production of technical effects during the second half of the twentieth century have noted that for many members of the mass audience, technical effects are persuasive for the same reasons that facts and statistics are. Just as we automatically associate data with knowledge, we tend to associate technology and technical effects with progress—that is, with the improvement of culture and society. President Clinton voiced this association in his 1996 State of the Union address when he associated the Age of Possibility with the growth of "technology, information, and global competition" (paragraph 7; see Chapter 5).

IBM exploited the association of technology and progress in a series of commercials that appeared frequently on National Football League telecasts in 1994 and 1995 and were featured during the 1995 Super Bowl. The series was entitled "Solutions for a Small Planet," and each commercial featured characters in a foreign country, talking in a non-English language (with English subtitles on the screen, as if it were a foreign movie) about the wonders of computer technology and how it had improved their lives. These characters were usually featured in settings not at all associated with technology: a nun talked about surfing the net while walking through a churchlike setting with other members of her religious order; two Middle Eastern men talked about business communication software in the middle of a dusty village; an Italian vineyard owner walked among his grapes, telling his daughter about how he earned his Ph.D. at Indiana University without ever leaving Italy by using his computer and modem. The overall message from the IBM series was that computer technology brings us all closer together, as we become a global community sharing communications hardware and software, while improving the quality of life, even for those who seem to live and work in quite nontechnological places.

The IBM series attempted to maintain the belief—what Aristotle might call a *maxim*—that technology is a force for positive change. By featuring technology and technical effects throughout its telecast, the 1996 Super Bowl reinforced this maxim and encouraged in the audience a positive identification with technology.

Through the interaction of *ethos, pathos,* and *kairos* and with a variety of appeals to identification and desire, the Super Bowl produces persuasion for millions—millions of dollars and millions of viewers! The nature of its appeals represents the psychology of mass culture in the United States, most especially the psychology of adult men, who make up the majority of the audience.

To Teach:
The *Ethos* of Graphic Information

A great deal of teaching goes on throughout the Super Bowl telecast, in terms of the delivery of information about the game and its players that viewers are unlikely or unable to find out for themselves. Here is a summary of the telecast features that comprise such teaching, each of which will be the focus of a subsequent section:

1. The onscreen display of statistics

2. Closeups of players, including comments on players' personal lives by announcers and attempts to reveal and identify with players' emotions or states of mind

3. Omniscient camera angles that suggest the scope and complexity of the event

4. Voyeurism: the camera eavesdropping on private activities

5. Emphasis on the wisdom and authority of announcers

As stated above, a main goal of persuasive teaching is to convince the audience that the material is worth knowing. In line with this goal, all of these Super Bowl teaching devices share a single purpose: to persuade the audience that the Super Bowl telecast is worth watching.

The Onscreen Display of Facts and Statistics: What Counts Is What Can Be Counted

In the 1996 Super Bowl, as Dallas Cowboys quarterback Troy Aikman took the field just after the opening kickoff, statistics that summarized his performance in past Super Bowls were flashed onto the screen: number of touchdowns, yards gained, and so forth. Just after the Cowboys scored the first points of the game, viewers saw in large letters at the bottom of the screen "SUPER BOWL FACT: Teams scoring first have won 21 of 29 games." Later in the first half of the game, a brief spot telecast between plays featured cartoon images of the players on the Dallas offensive line eating big plates of food, accompanied by statistics showing the weight of each player and finally the average weight of all the players on the line (333 pounds). At the beginning of the second half of play, viewers saw a statistical comparison of the performance of the opposing quarterbacks, featuring numbers of passes completed and attempted, yards gained, and touchdowns. And at many points throughout the game, closeups of players were accompanied by onscreen statistics tied to the current action.

Of course, featuring statistical data is common to all sports telecasts. During televised baseball games, onscreen icons keep us up to date on the counts of balls and strikes, which inning is in progress, and the score. Whenever a batter steps up to the plate, we are given his batting average and frequently other relevant data, such as his lifetime record against the opposing pitcher and his success rate with players on base. Statistics that are not displayed onscreen are often supplied by the announcers; it is not uncommon to hear an announcer say, for instance, "The last time Player X found himself batting in the bottom of the ninth with the bases loaded was on September 3, 1987, when he walked to drive in the winning run."

How do statistics function as elements of persuasion? While the central persuasive function of teaching is to feature the information as worth knowing, this information must first be accepted as true. Statistics tend to strike us as true because they seem to be impartial counts or measures, and while many of us know that collecting and presenting statistics can be biased, we don't tend to regard sports telecasts as occasions for statistical manipulation. If the network and announcers have any underlying purpose, we normally presume that it is to provide us, the audience, full and comprehensive enjoyment of the game; we regard the display of statistics as contributing to our full enjoyment. In other words, the onscreen display of statistics is part of an *ethos* of goodwill, in part because statistics don't appear to be selling us anything.

On the other hand, to the extent that we presume that a presentation wants to move us or sell us something, we are suspicious of the validity of the facts and statistics presented; that is, we are suspicious of the *ethos* of the presentation. Suppose a political ad flashes on the TV screen, saying, "Candidate Y voted against capital punishment 17 times in the last 10 years. Candidate Y is soft on crime. Vote for Candidate X." Many viewers will conclude that the purpose of this ad is to move voters and will neither presume goodwill nor statistical objectivity on the part of the advertiser (especially in view of the wide critical publicity recently given to negative campaigning). Also, viewers will tend to regard this political spot as a kind of commercial, which, like all commercials, is calculated to move the audience, to change their minds and influence their behaviors, to sell a product (in this case, Candidate X).

Once again, for persuasive teaching to be fully effective, the Super Bowl statistics must be regarded not only as true (impartial and objective) but also as worth knowing. Many people regard knowing facts and statistics as inherently worthwhile because they hold what educational theorist Paulo Freire has called a *banking theory* of knowledge. We have all had years of schooling in which a good memory for data was rewarded with high test scores; we have been conditioned, according to the Freirean view, to think of knowledge as something that is deposited (like money), in the form of data, into our minds (which serve as banks). Apart from schooling, our culture generally values the knowledge of data, as is evident from the popularity of games such as *Trivial Pursuit* and *Jeopardy.* In general, then, we tend to associate knowledge with quantity of information. In this connection, we often associate knowing a person with knowing statistics about him or her. Here is a description of Johnny Carson, former host of *The Tonight Show,* taken from *The National Enquirer:*

> Johnny has asked his guests more than 110,000 questions over the past 30 years. Some 83 guest hosts have taken Johnny's seat. More than three million people have sat in the audience at "Tonight Show" tapings. . . . Last year he earned $2,380 for each minute on the air. (19 May 1992, p. 20)

(*TV Guide* and *The National Enquirer* are the most popular weekly magazines in the world, and both are filled with numerical facts and statistics.)

In the Super Bowl, knowing a player means knowing biographical facts and statistics about him. So when Jay Novacek scored the first touchdown for Dallas, we were treated to a closeup of his face as he walked off the field, accompanied by the announcer's summary of Novacek's biographical data: his birthplace, college education, and years with the Cowboys. The combination of a closeup plus brief facts is the television sports equivalent of getting to know someone, or put another way, of *teaching* us who he is. The Novacek image contributes to the general persuasive purpose of the whole telecast, which is to convince us that the telecast itself is worth watching. When a statistic appears on the screen, it initiates a syllogism that may be shared by many members of the audience:

> Numerical facts increase my knowledge.
>
> This telecast features numerical facts.
>
> This telecast increases my knowledge.

Closeups of Players: Getting Personal

Besides delivering an extensive battery of facts and statistics, sports announcers maintain a positive *ethos* by stressing their familiarity with the personal lives of the players and involving us in that familiarity through visual closeups and personal anecdotes. A closeup is often accompanied by some brief narrative about the player's personal or professional life, as with the brief biography of Novacek delivered just after his first touchdown. At another point in the 1996 Super Bowl, an announcer narrated a closeup of Steelers quarterback Neil O'Donnell by saying that he came from a big family and that his father gave him the nickname "Super Baby" early in life.

Such moments work not only to maintain our sense of the announcer's authoritative grasp of a great range of information connected with the game and its players but also to engage us in some identification with the players themselves. As noted earlier, viewer identification with the players contributes to the pleasing quality of the telecast. The announcers add to this pleasure by teaching us something personal about a player at the same time that they bring an image of that player up close. The creation of familiarity makes the player seem more like us, as in cases when a closeup is accompanied by the announcer suggesting the player's humble origins: "Player Y grew up on a farm in Peoria, Illinois, and used to practice pitching by throwing at a target on the side of a barn." Such anecdotes about the personal lives of players are common in all sports telecasts, along with occasional camera shots of the players' family members in the stadium audience.

Sometimes identification is encouraged by disclosing the player's emotions. A closeup of a key player usually follows a significantly successful or unsuccessful play: a batter walking to the dugout after striking out or after hitting a home run; a pitcher just after giving up a home run; a basketball player who has just committed a personal foul; a quarterback who has just been sacked; a receiver who has just scored a touchdown. Each of these images usually tries to disclose some emotional response from the player: the frustrated batter hurling his batting helmet into the dugout; the exuberant receiver smiling broadly and raising his arms in celebration. And typically, the announcer delivers some comment about the emotional state of the player. At one point during the second half of the 1996 Super Bowl, after Steelers quarterback Neil O'Donnell had executed a series of unsuccessful plays, the camera revealed the frustration in his face and an announcer said, "Just settle down, Neil." The announcer acted as a teacher here by showing us— through the technical resources of the telecast—visual information about the game that would otherwise be invisible. In this way, the announcer reinforces the *ethos* of his practical wisdom by demonstrating that he sees and knows more than we do; in addition, the announcer maintains his goodwill by allowing us to share his view and reinforces pleasure through identification by stressing that O'Donnell can get frustrated, just like the rest of us.

Omniscient Camera Angles:
The *Ethos* of the All-Seeing Eye

So far, we have looked at the ways in which the *ethos* of practical wisdom and goodwill is maintained by devices such as onscreen statistics and closeups. Practical wisdom is also emphasized by the continual impression that the Super Bowl is too big and complicated an event to comprehend without the help of the network's announcers and technologies. As rhetorical theorist Barry Brummett (mentioned earlier) points out, football telecasts consist largely of scattered visual images and fast-moving action. For this reason, they employ various devices to give what might otherwise seem a fragmented and confusing scene some unity and meaning. These devices include:

1. Multiple camera positions, from extreme closeups to extreme long shots (taken from blimps) as well as shots of the stadium crowd, the coaches, the players on the bench, and the line of scrimmage—all conveying the impression that the viewer is enjoying a comprehensive experience that would be impossible except for the medium of television

2. A slow-motion replay of every play, accompanied by the announcer's recapitulation of the action and analysis of the reasons for its success or failure (often using "chalk diagrams" drawn onscreen)

3. Frequent summaries that bring viewers up to date on the progress of the game

4. Indications of relevant events off the field (for instance, just after the beginning of the 1996 game, we were told by the announcers that because the field was slippery, a number of the Dallas Cowboys had changed their shoes)

5. The repeated display and announcement of player and game statistics

Voyeurism:
Eavesdropping on Private Activities

Brummett also notes that sports telecasts typically appeal to our *voyeurism,* or the sense that we are watching a private moment. This is part of the effect of closeups of players at crucial moments in the game. The technology of voyeurism was apparent in the 1996 Super Bowl when we watched a replay of the wife of the Steelers head coach and her daughter, viewing the game from their stadium seats and reacting to a Steelers touchdown that had just occurred; they were elated, screaming and embracing. A camera had been recording them while we were watching other live action, and the replay gave the impression that cameras in a number of places were eavesdropping on individuals in the game. The eavesdropping cameras were apparent in a number of shots: a corpulent man with a big cowboy hat among the spectators; occasional glimpses of the Dallas Cowboy Cheerleaders; Cowboys coach Barry Switzer, wearing a hidden microphone and "overheard" saying "I love ya, I love ya" to his players as he entered the field.

Such voyeuristic observations are very common in sports telecasts, especially those of baseball games; the slower pace of baseball allows for frequent shots of people in the stands, between batters, between pitches, and so forth. Such shots maintain the sports telecast's effective *ethos* by suggesting *omniscience,* that is, the network's full command of all the action, on and off the field. Because the network can see so much, we are persuaded to regard its wisdom and authority as ultimate.

The Wisdom and Authority of Announcers:
The Network Team Knows Best

In the Super Bowl, the practical wisdom of the announcers is reinforced by stressing their special knowledge of the game. For instance, the 1996 telecast used Dick Enberg, a seasoned sports announcer, and Phil Simms, a former Super Bowl player, along with halftime commentators Joe Montana, another former bowl player, and two very successful coaches, Mike Ditka and Joe Gibbs. In short, the 1996 presentation of the Super Bowl met two of the most important elements of persuasive teaching:

1. The created impression that the teachers (in this case, the announcers and network technologies) are indispensable to full understanding

2. The featuring of the teachers as uniquely qualified and authoritative, as people who tell the truth

Teaching in the TV Emergency Room

As another instance of television teaching at work, we might consider one of the most popular prime-time, nonsports programs on the air: *ER*. This drama is set in the emergency room of a Chicago public hospital, where an ensemble cast—portraying physicians, nurses, and support staff—handles a wide variety of often life-threatening medical cases in each episode. In addition, these main characters must deal with the trials and traumas of their own professional and personal lives.

The popularity of *ER* corresponds with the current popularity of programs and TV movies that dramatize medical, legal, and social problems (for instance, AIDS, child custody conflicts, abortion rights, sexual harassment) and attempt to teach the viewing audience about the issue or problem in question. *ER* teaches about emergency room medicine and medical practice in general, mainly by providing fairly complete and sometimes graphic portrayals of the conditions of the patients and possible treatments and cures. When Anthony Edwards, as Dr. Mark Greene, talks to a patient about how to deal with her cervical cancer, he is both acting his part and teaching the viewing audience something about the disease. Remember that for teaching to be persuasive, the student (or audience) must regard the information as both authoritative and worth learning. By creating what many regard as realistic settings and conditions and through frequently using clinical language in the dialogue, *ER* attempts to maintain an *ethos* of authority.

Further, the information *ER* teaches is almost certain to be regarded as worth knowing because it concerns accidents and diseases to which we all feel vulnerable. In fact, a group of doctors has published a study in which they worry that viewers are accepting as accurate what are really inaccurate portrayals of medical emergencies on TV shows such as *ER, Chicago Hope,* and *Rescue 911*. In the spring of 1996, Dr. James Tulsky and his associates reported that these programs were not portraying pulmonary resuscitation correctly and emphasized that in reality that procedure is both more gruesome and less successful than television representations suggest (*New England Journal of Medicine,* 13 June 1996). In other words, these teaching shows create a persuasive *ethos* for viewers but one that may not represent the real world.

Summary

The National Football League's Super Bowl is a tremendously popular television event that employs a number of different persuasive strategies in order to teach, please, and move its audience. The 1996 Super Bowl concentrated its efforts on pleasing the audience in the halftime show. In line with Aristotelian conceptions of *pathos,* the halftime show reflected the desires, experiences, and beliefs of the large baby-boomer sector of the television audience. To appeal to the audience's nostalgia, the halftime show featured Diana Ross, whose recordings were most popular during the 1970s and would be immediately familiar to that baby-boomer audience. Ross's show encouraged the audience's pleasurable identification with their own past and, by transporting them to that past, offered them an alternative reality. The spectacle of the halftime show also created an alternative reality through magical and fantastic special effects. Besides nostalgia and spectacle, the halftime show also appealed to the audience's desire for love through a medley of love songs and onfield demonstrations of harmony and community.

The Super Bowl halftime show, which emphasized love, sharply contrasted the game itself, which featured violent agression and may have encouraged audience identification with hate, rather than love. We can think of the halftime show as a disruption of the logical or syllogistic form of the Super Bowl, or with reference to Kenneth Burke's concept of *qualitative form,* we can think of the halftime show as a kind of relief from the mood of the game itself. However, an audience that does not notice the contradictions between the game and the halftime show may have been conditioned not to exercise critical consciousness when watching television.

While a central purpose of the 1996 halftime show may have been to please the audience, the purpose of the commercials shown during the Super Bowl (and of commercials in general) was to move the audience to buy certain products. The arrangement of commercials during the game often corresponded to predictable desires on the part of the audience; for instance, food commercials were more numerous very early in the game, when viewers were more likely to be making decisions about what to eat. Further, the Super Bowl commercials were full of high-tech special effects, thus appealing to an audience that identifies technology with progress and that enjoys a positive identification with demonstrations of technology's power.

A third purpose of the Super Bowl telecast, to teach, was evident mainly in the presentation of statistical data throughout the game by the announcers and through onscreen displays. By giving the audience special knowledge about the players and teams and by using sophisticated camera work to reveal details of the event that would otherwise remain unnoticed, the telecast maintained an *ethos* of great authority. Because the telecast provided apparently significant information about the game and its players that was not available elsewhere, viewers tended to be persuaded that the telecast was the ultimate Super Bowl authority and worth watching if only because it increased their storehouse of facts and let them see what stadium spectators could not.

❖ *Questions to Ask Yourself*

1. Is it possible to exercise what the author calls *critical consciousness* about a sports telecast (that is, to notice its elements of persuasion) and still remain a sports fan? How so?

2. In this chapter, by focusing on the Super Bowl, does the author appeal to the interest of male readers more than female readers? Might some sections of the discussion appeal to the interests of women more than men? Explain your answers.

3. The description of the halftime show (pp. 96–97) is *selective*, rather than *comprehensive*. That is, the author focuses mainly on those characteristics of the show that are relevant to his analysis and does not describe in detail every moment of the show. Given this, how do you know that the author is not leaving out aspects of the show that would weaken his analysis? In other words, what reasons do you have for accepting and trusting his description?

❖ *Writing Exercise*

How are the persuasive strategies associated with the 1996 Super Bowl adapted to other kinds of television programs? You might watch a half-hour situation comedy, commercials and all, and ask how the plot or dialogue serves to teach; what desires, beliefs, and values the show appeals to in order to please; and how its commercials might be especially appropriate to move its television audience. What about Saturday morning cartoon shows? News broadcasts? Talk shows? You may want to focus on just one kind of program or compare several different kinds.

❖ *Persuasive Strategies for Student Writers*

1. How and where does your writing offer your audience an alternative reality? For instance, if you are writing in order to persuade your readers to use public transportation instead of driving their own cars, the alternative reality you offer would be highways with less traffic, cleaner air, and so forth. If you are writing to describe a significant personal experience, your account of it can constitute a reality that your readers have not themselves experienced. If you are writing to analyze the elements of persuasion in certain television programs, are you offering readers an alternative to their normal viewing habits or choices? How so?

2. Employing the concept of *kairos* means having some control over the timing of a presentation to an audience. Is it possible to exercise any control over the timing of the statements in your writing? If you offer several examples to support your main point, ask yourself which you should state first, second, third, and so on. Why?

3. This chapter suggests that facts and statistics can supply useful, relevant knowledge but sometimes only *seem* to do so. Which of the facts and statistics in your writing are necessary and relevant? Why?

5

Persuasion in the Political Scene

The State of the Union Address

This is not a State of the Union message. It's a formal announcement of his agenda to run for re-election.

> —John Forst, a Des Moines, Iowa, travel agency manager, while watching President Clinton deliver the 1996 State of the Union address (*Chicago Tribune*, 24 Jan. 1996, p. 1)

I feel there is nothing that can be done about anything.

> —Carmen Rios, a cosmetology instructor who decided not to watch the speech (*Chicago Tribune*, 24 Jan. 1996, p. 1)

Every January, the President of the United States addresses a joint session of Congress on the State of the Union. In doing so, the president carries out the responsibility mandated in the U.S. Constitution: "[The president] shall from time to time give to the Congress information of the state of the Union, and recommend to their consideration such measures as he shall judge necessary and expedient." President William Jefferson Clinton delivered his fourth State of the Union address on

Tuesday, January 23, 1996, to a joint session of Congress, the president's cabinet, the justices of the Supreme Court, a gallery of observers (including First Lady Hillary Rodham Clinton and the Clintons' daughter, Chelsea), and a national audience watching on television and listening on radio. This speech embodied the typical motives of many of its predecessors: The president was attempting to convince Congress to support an agenda of policies and legislation and to influence public opinion in favor of this agenda, as well. But the speech was also distinctive, as it was connected to the particular circumstances and problems facing Clinton at the time, and representative of how a persuasion event can and must illustrate a complex set of motives, purposes, and circumstances and appeal to a range of different audiences.

In late January 1996, Clinton was just a little over nine months away from election day, when his bid for a second term would either succeed or fail. He was a Democratic president contending with a Republican Congress, a Congress that had gained that Republican majority a year earlier, largely due to the power and popularity of the man who sat behind the president as he spoke, Speaker of the House Newt Gingrich. But in the weeks just preceding the State of the Union address, this Democratic president and Republican Congress had been engaged in a series of battles over balancing the federal budget, leading to an impasse that resulted in closing federal offices and temporarily suspending pay to federal employees. In this conflict, the Republicans were generally perceived (according to public opinion polls) as bearing most of the responsibility for the closure of government offices and the hardship this caused, while Clinton was perceived as both strong and compassionate; his approval rating rose, while that of Gingrich and the Republican leadership fell. Polls taken just prior to the State of the Union address suggested that the majority of the general public that the president faced on this night was largely conservative. A poll broadcast by CNN on January 23, 1996, indicated that 60 percent of those polled thought government should promote traditional values. Apart from party politics, President Clinton also had other problems in January 1996 that affected his public image: He had been named in a sexual harassment suit, alleging impropriety on his part while he was Governor of Arkansas, and his wife, Hillary Rodham Clinton, had (on the very day of the address, January 23) been subpoenaed by a federal grand jury to answer questions about her possible involvement in the cover-up of an illegal investment scheme, in which the president had also been implicated.

In this chapter, we will survey the 1996 State of the Union address in its entirety, noting instances of the elements of persuasion we have covered so far in this book and introducing others that are particularly relevant to this mode of political persuasion.

In order to understand the version of the speech we will examine in this chapter, keep in mind that the State of the Union address is released in a printed version shortly before the president actually delivers it. Thus, the spoken version differs from the written version; it includes minor changes in wording and sentence structure, as well as some substantial revisions and additions. Using the predelivery written version of Clinton's 1996 address as our basic text, I have indicated the changes appearing in the spoken version as follows:

- Words within parentheses ( ) are *additions* to the written version.

- Words within curved brackets { } are *deletions* from the written version.

- Words within square brackets [ ] are *substitutions* to the written version.

Noticing these changes will allow us to consider the possible reasons behind some of them.

Because applause is often an indicator of the persuasive effect of a speech, we will want to consider its function during the president's address. Clinton's 1996 speech was interrupted 74 times with applause; in our text, each instance is indicated by *APPLAUSE*.

Each paragraph of the speech is numbered at the beginning using a number within triangular brackets < >. This will make it easier for you to locate particular passages cited in our later discussion.

In order to present a summary of the elements of persuasion we have treated in this book and to indicate the ways in which a full text can be analyzed in these terms, we will first read the entire State of the Union address. Then later in the chapter, we will discuss how *ethos, pathos, logos,* speech acts, dramatism, and identification are at work throughout the speech.

Text of the
1996 State of the Union Address

<1>   Mr. Speaker, Mr. Vice President, Members of the 104th
Congress, distinguished guests, my fellow Americans all
across our land.

<2>   {I want to} [let me] begin (tonight) by saying to our men
and women in uniform around the world, and especially those
helping peace take root in Bosnia, and to their families, thank
you. America is very (very) proud of you. *APPLAUSE*

<3>   My duty tonight is to report on the State of the Union, not
the state of our government but of our American community,
and to set forth our responsibilities—in the words of our
Founders—to "form a more perfect union."

<4>   The State of the Union is strong. Our economy is the
healthiest it has been in three decades. *APPLAUSE, beginning
and growing from "strong."* We have the lowest combined rate
of unemployment and inflation in 27 years.

<5>   We have created nearly 8 million new jobs, over a million
of them in basic industries like construction and automobiles.
America is selling more cars than Japan for the first time
since the 1970s, and for three years in a row we have had a
record number of new businesses started (in our country).
APPLAUSE

<6>   Our leadership in the world is also strong, bringing {new
hope for} [hope for new] peace. And perhaps most important,
we are gaining ground in restoring our fundamental values.
The crime rate, the welfare and food stamp rolls, the poverty
rate, and the teen pregnancy rate are all down. And as they
go down, prospects for America's future go up. *APPLAUSE*

<7>   We live in an Age of Possibility. A hundred years ago
we moved from farm to factory. Now we move to an age of
technology, information, and global competition.

<8>   These changes have opened vast new opportunities (for
our people), but they {also present} [have also presented]
(them with) stiff challenges. While more Americans are living
better {lives}, too many of our fellow citizens are working

harder just to keep up. And they are (rightly) concerned about the security of their families.

<9>   We must answer (here) three fundamental questions: (First) How do we make the American dream of opportunity (for all) a reality for all (Americans) who are willing to work for it? (Second) How do we preserve our old and enduring values as we move into the future? And (third) how do we meet these challenges together, as one America?

<10>   We know big government does not have all the answers. (We know) There is not a program for every problem. *APPLAUSE, beginning at "answers."* We know {we need} [and we have worked to give the American people] a smaller, less bureaucratic government in Washington—(and we have to give the American people) one that lives within its means. *APPLAUSE*

<11>   The era of big government is over. *APPLAUSE* But we cannot go back to the time when our citizens were left to fend for themselves. *APPLAUSE*

<12>   Instead, we must go forward as one America—one nation working together, to meet the challenges we face together. Self reliance and teamwork are not opposing virtues—we must have both. *APPLAUSE*

<13>   I believe our new, smaller government must work in an old-fashioned American way—together with all our citizens, through state and local governments, in the workplace, in religious, charitable, and civic associations.

<14>   Our goal must be: to enable all our people to make the most of their own lives with stronger families, more educational opportunity, economic security, safer streets, a cleaner environment, (and) a safer world.

<15>   To improve the state of our union, we must all ask more of ourselves; we must expect more of each other; and we must face our challenges together. *APPLAUSE* [Here in this place] Our responsibility {here} begins with balancing the budget in a way that is fair to all Americans. *APPLAUSE* There is now broad bipartisan agreement that permanent deficit spending must come to an end. *APPLAUSE*

<16>   I compliment the {Republicans} [Republican leadership and the membership] for the energy and determination {they} [you] have brought to this task (of balancing the budget). *APPLAUSE* And I thank the Democrats for passing the largest deficit reduction plan in history in 1993, which has already cut the deficit nearly in half in {just} three years. *APPLAUSE*

<17>   Since {then} [1993], we have all begun to see the benefits of deficit reduction: lower interest rates have made it easier for {business} [businesses to borrow, and to invest and] to create new jobs. {and} [Lower interest rates] have brought down the cost of home mortgages, car payments and credit card rates to ordinary citizens. Now it is time to finish the job (and balance the budget). *APPLAUSE* Though differences remain among us (that are significant), the combined total of the proposed savings common to both plans is more than enough, using numbers from your Congressional Budget Office, to balance the budget in seven years and to provide a modest tax cut. These cuts are real; they will require sacrifice from everyone.

<18>   But these cuts do not undermine our fundamental obligations to our parents, our children, and our future by endangering Medicare, (or) Medicaid, (or) education or the environment, or by raising taxes on {the hardest pressed} working families. *APPLAUSE*

<19>   (I have said before and let me say again, many good ideas have come out of our negotiations. I have learned a lot about the way both Republicans and Democrats view the debate before us. I have learned a lot about the good ideas that each side has that we could embrace.) {I am willing to work} [We ought] to resolve our remaining differences. (I am willing to work to resolve them.) I am ready to meet tomorrow. But I ask you (to consider that we should) at least to enact these savings {so we can} [that both plans have in common, and] give the American people their balanced budget, a tax cut, lower interest rates and a brighter future.

<20>   We {must} [should do that now, and] make permanent deficits yesterday's legacy. *APPLAUSE*

<21>   Now it is time (for us) to look (also) to the challenges
of today and tomorrow (beyond the burdens of yesterday).
(The challenges are significant, but) Our nation was built on
challenges, not promises. (America was built on challenges,
not promises.) When we work together to meet them, we
never fail. That is the key to a more perfect union: our
individual dreams must be realized by our common efforts.

<22>   Tonight, I want to speak about the challenges we (all)
face as a people. Our first challenge is to cherish our children
and strengthen {American} [America's] families. Families are
the foundation of American life. If we have stronger families,
we will have a stronger {nation} [America].

<23>   (Before I go on, I'd like to take just a moment to thank my
own family, and to thank the person who's taught me more
than anyone else over twenty-five years about the importance
of families and children. A wonderful wife, a magnificent
mother, and a great First Lady. Thank you, Hillary.)
APPLAUSE

<24>   Strong families begin with taking more responsibility for
our children. (I've heard Mrs. Gore say that) It is hard to be a
parent today; but it is even harder to be a child. (So) All of
us—{our parents,} [not just as parents, but all of us in our
other roles—] our media, our schools, our teachers, our communities, our churches (and synagogues), our businesses,
and government—(all of us) have a responsibility to help
children (to) make it (and to make the most of their lives,
and their God-given capacities).

<25>   To the media: I say you should create movies, (and) CDs
and television shows you would want your own children and
grandchildren to enjoy. *APPLAUSE* I call on Congress to pass
the requirement for a "V" chip in TV sets, so (that) parents
can screen out programs {which} they believe are inappropriate for their {younger} children. *APPLAUSE* When parents
control what their (young) children see, that's not censorship.
That's enabling parents to assume more (personal) responsibility for their {children} [children's upbringing]. And I
urge them to do it. The "V" chip requirement is part of the

(important) telecommunications bill now pending (in this Congress). It has bipartisan support, and I urge you to pass it now. *APPLAUSE*

<26>   To make the "V" chip work, I challenge the broadcast industry to do what movies have done, to identify your programming in ways that help parents (to) protect their children.

<27>   (And) I invite the leaders of major media corporations and the entertainment industry to come to the White House next month to work with us (in a positive way) on concrete ways to improve what our children see on television. I am ready to work with you. *APPLAUSE*

<28>   I say to those who make and market cigarettes: Every year a million children take up smoking (even though it's against the law); 300,000 of them will have their lives shortened as a result. {My} [Our] administration has taken steps to stop the massive marketing {campaign} [campaigns] that {appeals} [appeal] to our children. We are (simply) saying: Market your products to adults, if you wish—but draw the line on children. *APPLAUSE*

<29>   I say to those (who are) on welfare (and especially to those who have been trapped on welfare for a long time): For too long, our welfare system has undermined the values of family and work, instead of supporting them. (The) Congress and I are near agreement on sweeping welfare reform.

<30>   We agree on time limits, tough work requirements, and the toughest possible child support enforcement. But (I believe) we must also provide child care so that mothers {can go to work} [who are required to go to work can do so] without worrying about (what is happening to) their children. *APPLAUSE* {So} I challenge (this) Congress: (to) Send me a bipartisan welfare reform bill that will really move people from welfare to work and do (the) right (thing) by our children, {and} I will sign it. *APPLAUSE*

<31>   But (let us be candid about this difficult problem:) passing a law (even the best possible law) is only {the} [a] first step. The next step is to make it work. I challenge people

on welfare to make the most of this opportunity for independence. {And} I challenge American business to give {them}
[people on welfare] a chance to move {from welfare to work}
[into the workforce]. I applaud the work of religious groups
{that} [and others who] care for the poor.

<32>   More than anyone else, they know the (true) difficulty of
{this} [the] task (before us), and they are in a position to help.
Every one of us should join with them. (That is the only way
we can make real welfare reform a reality in the lives of the
American people.)

<33>   To strengthen the family, we must do everything we can
to keep the teen pregnancy rate going down. (I am gratified
as I am sure all Americans are, that it has dropped for two
years in a row. But we all know) It is still far too high. Tonight I am pleased to announce that a group of prominent
Americans is responding to that challenge by forming an
organization that will support grass roots community efforts
(all across our country) in a national campaign against teen
pregnancy. And I challenge (all of us and) every American to
join {them} [their efforts].

<34>   I call on American men and women (in families) to (give
greater) respect (to) one another. We must end the deadly
scourge of domestic violence (in our country). *APPLAUSE*
(And) I challenge America's families to (work harder to) stay
together (for families that stay together not only do better
economically, their children do better, as well).

<35>   In particular, I challenge (the) fathers (of this country) to
love and care for their children. If your family has separated,
you must pay your child support. We are doing more than
ever to make sure you do, and we are going to do more. But
let's all admit (something about that too): A check will never
{be a} substitute for a {father's} [parent's] love and guidance,
and only you can make the decision to help raise your
children—no matter who you are, (how low or high your
station in life,) it is {your} [the] most basic human duty (of
every American to do that job to the best of his or her ability).
APPLAUSE

<36>   Our second challenge is to provide Americans with the educational opportunities {we} [we'll all] need for {a} [this] new century.

<37>   (In our schools) Every classroom in America must be connected to the information superhighway, with computers, (and) good software, and well-trained teachers. We are working with the telecommunications industry, educators and parents to connect 20 percent of {the} [California's] classrooms {in California} by this spring, and every classroom and library in {America} [the entire United States] by the year 2000. *APPLAUSE* I ask Congress to support our education technology initiative {to} [so that we can] make (sure) this national partnership {successful} [succeeds].

<38>   Every diploma ought to mean something. I challenge every community, (every) school and (every) state to adopt national standards of excellence, (to) measure whether schools are meeting those standards, (to) cut (bureaucratic) red tape so that schools (and teachers)have more flexibility for grassroots reform, and hold them accountable for results. That's what our Goals 2000 initiative is all about.

<39>   I challenge every state to give all parents the right to choose which public school their children (will) attend, and (to) let teachers form new schools with a charter they can keep only if they do a good job. *APPLAUSE*

<40>   I challenge all (our) schools to teach character education: (to teach) good values, and good citizenship. And if it means teenagers will stop killing each other over designer jackets, then (our) public schools should be able to require (their students to wear) school uniforms. *APPLAUSE*

<41>   I challenge parents to {be} [become] their children's first teachers. Turn off the TV. See that the homework gets done. (And) Visit your children's classroom. (No program, no teacher, no one else can do that for you.)

<42>   {Today} [My fellow Americans], higher education is more important (today) than ever before. We have created a new student loan program that has made it easier to borrow and repay (those) loans; and (we have) dramatically cut the student loan default rate. (That's something we should all

be proud of, because it was unconscionably high just a few years ago.) Through AmeriCorps, our national service program, this year 25,000 students will earn college money by serving {in} their local communities (to improve the lives of their friends and neighbors). *APPLAUSE* These initiatives are right for America; (and) we should keep them going.

<43>   And we should (also work hard to) open the doors {to} [of] college even wider. I challenge Congress to expand work study and help one million young Americans work their way through college by the year 2000; to provide a $1,000 merit scholarship for the top 5 percent of graduates in every high school (in the United States) *APPLAUSE;* to expand Pell Grant scholarships for deserving (and needy) students; and to make up to $10,000 a year of college tuition tax deductible. *APPLAUSE*

<44>   Our third challenge is to help every American (who is willing to work for it) achieve economic security (in this new age).

<45>   People who work hard still need support to get ahead in the new economy—(they need) education and training for a lifetime, (they need) more support for families raising children, (they need) retirement security, and (they need) access to health care.

<46>   More and more Americans are finding that the education of their childhood simply does not last a lifetime.

<47>   (So) I challenge Congress to consolidate 70 overlapping (antiquated) job training programs into a simple voucher worth $2,600 for unemployed or underemployed workers to use (as they please) for community college tuition or other training. {Pass} this [is a] GI Bill for America's Workers we should all be able to agree on. *APPLAUSE*

<48>   More and more Americans are working hard without a raise. Congress sets the minimum wage. Within a year, the minimum wage will fall to a 40-year low in purchasing power. $4.25 an hour is {not a living wage} [no longer a minimum]. But millions of Americans and their children are trying to live on it. I challenge you to raise their minimum wage. *APPLAUSE*

<49>   In 1993, Congress cut the taxes of 15 million hard-pressed working families, to make sure (that) no parents who worked full-time would have to raise their children in poverty (and to encourage people to move from welfare to work). This expanded Earned Income Tax Credit is now worth about $1,800 a year to a family of four living on $20,000. The budget bill I vetoed would have reversed this achievement, and raised taxes on nearly 8 million of these people. We {must} [should] not do that (We should not do that). *APPLAUSE*

<50>   (But I also agree that the people who are helped under this initiative are not all those in our country who are working hard to do a good job raising their children and at work. I agree that) We need a tax credit for working families with children. That's one (of the) thing(s) most of us in this chamber can (I hope) agree on. (I know it is strongly supported by the Republican majority) And it should be part of any final budget agreement. *APPLAUSE*

<51>   I (want to) challenge every business that can possibly afford it to provide pensions for your employees, and I challenge Congress to pass a proposal recommended by the White House Conference on Small Business, that would make it easier for small businesses and farmers to establish their own pension plans. (That is something we should all agree on.) *APPLAUSE*

<52>   We should also protect existing pension plans. Two years ago, with bipartisan support (that was almost unanimous on both sides of the aisle), we {protected} [moved to protect] the pensions of 8 million working people and {stabilized} [to stabilize] the pensions of 32 million more. Congress should not now let companies endanger {their} [those] workers' pension funds. (I know the proposal to liberalize the ability of employers to take money out of pension funds for other purposes would raise money for the treasury. But I believe it is false economy.) I vetoed {such a} [that] proposal last year, and I would {veto it} [have to do so] again. *APPLAUSE*

<53>   Finally, if (our) working families are going to succeed in the new economy, they must be able to buy health insurance policies that they don't lose when they change jobs or when

someone in their family gets sick. Over the past 2 years, over 1 million Americans in working families (have) lost their health insurance. We must do more to make health care available to every American. And Congress should start by passing the bipartisan bill {before you} [sponsored by Senator Kennedy and Senator Kassebaum] that {requires} [would require] insurance companies to stop dropping people when they switch jobs, and stop denying coverage for preexisting conditions. (Let's all do that.) *APPLAUSE*

<54>   And {we must} [even as we enact savings in these programs, we must have the common commitment to] preserve the basic protections Medicare and Medicaid give, not just to the poor, but to people in working families, including children, people with disabilities, people with AIDS, {and} senior citizens in nursing homes. In the past 3 years we have saved $15 billion just by fighting health care fraud and abuse. We {can} [have all agreed to] save much more. (We have all agreed to stabilize the Medicare trust fund) But we {cannot} [must not] abandon our fundamental obligations to the people who need Medicare and Medicaid. America cannot become stronger if they become weaker. *APPLAUSE*

<55>   The GI Bill for Workers, tax relief for education and child rearing, pension availability and protection, access to health care, preservation of Medicare and Medicaid, these things along with the Family and Medical Leave Act passed in 1993—(these things) will help responsible hard-working American families to make the most of their own lives.

<56>   But, employers and employees must do their part as well, as they are (doing) in so many of our finest companies, working together, putting (the) long-term prosperity ahead of (the) short-term gains.

<57>   As workers increase their hours and their productivity, employers should make sure they get the skills they need and share the benefits of the good years as well as the burdens of the bad ones. When companies and workers work as a team, they do better. And so does America.

<58>   Our fourth great challenge is to take {back} our streets [back] from crime, (and) gangs, and drugs.

<59>   At last, we have begun to find the way to reduce crime—forming community partnerships with local police forces to catch criminals and to prevent crime. This strategy, called community policing, {has begun to work} [is clearly working]. Violent crime is coming down all across America.

<60>   In New York City, murders are down 25 percent, in St. Louis 18 percent, in Seattle 32 percent. But we still have a long way to go before our streets are safe and our people are free {of} [from] fear.

<61>   The Crime Bill of 1994 is critical to the success of community policing. It provides funds for 100,000 new police in communities of all sizes. We are already a third of the way there. (And) I challenge the Congress to finish the job. Let's stick with a strategy that's working, and keep the crime rate coming down. *APPLAUSE*

<62>   Community policing also requires bonds of trust be-tween {our} citizens and {our} police. So I ask all Americans to respect and support our {police} [law enforcement officers]. And to our police, I say: Our children need you as role models and heroes. Don't let them down.

<63>   The Brady Bill has already stopped 44,000 people with criminal records from buying guns. The assault weapons ban is keeping 19 kinds of assault weapons out of the hands of violent gangs. I challenge (the) Congress to keep those laws on the books. *APPLAUSE*

<64>   Our next step in the fight against crime is to take on gangs the way we (once) took on the mob. I am directing the FBI and other investigative agencies to target gangs that involve juveniles in violent crime and to seek authority to prosecute as adults teenagers who maim and kill like adults.

<65>   And I challenge local housing authorities and tenant associations: Criminal gang members and drug dealers are destroying the lives of decent tenants. From now on, the rule for residents who commit crimes and peddle drugs should be: one strike and you're out. *APPLAUSE*

<66>   I challenge every state to match federal policy: to assure that serious violent criminals serve at least 85 percent of their sentence. *APPLAUSE* More police and punishment are

important, but (they're) not enough. We {must} [have got to] keep more of our young people out of trouble, with prevention strategies not dictated by Washington, but developed in communities. I challenge all (of our) communities {and} (all of our) adults to give {these} [our] children futures to say yes to. And I challenge Congress not to abandon the Crime Bill's support of these grassroots (prevention) efforts. *APPLAUSE*

<67>   Finally, to reduce crime and violence, we {must} [have to] reduce the drug problem. The challenge begins {at} [in our] {home} [homes], with parents talking to their children openly and firmly. It embraces our churches (and synagogues, our) youth groups, and our schools.

<68>   I challenge Congress not to cut our support for drug-free schools. People like (these) D.A.R.E. officers are making an impression on grade school children that will give them the strength to say no when the time comes. *APPLAUSE* Meanwhile, we continue our efforts to cut the flow of drugs into America. For the last two years, one man in particular has been on the front-lines of that effort. {And} tonight I am nominating (him,) a hero of the Persian Gulf and the commander-in-chief of the U.S. Military's Southern Command, General Barry McCaffrey, as America's new drug czar. *APPLAUSE*

<69>   General McCaffrey has earned three purple hearts and two silver stars fighting for {America} [this country]. Tonight I ask that he lead our nation's battle against drugs at home and abroad.

<70>   To succeed, he needs a force (far) larger than he has ever commanded. He needs all of us. Every one of us {will} have a role to play on this team. Thank you, General McCaffrey, for agreeing to serve your country one more time. *APPLAUSE*

<71>   Our fifth challenge {is} to leave our environment safe and clean for the next generation.

<72>   Because of a generation of bipartisan effort, we (do) have cleaner air and water. Lead levels in children's blood has been cut by 70 percent, and toxic emissions from factories cut in half. Lake Erie was dead. (And) Now it is a thriving resource.

<73>   But 10 million children under 12 still live within four
miles of a toxic waste dump. A third of us breathe air {which}
[that] endangers our health. And in too many communities,
(the) water is not safe to drink. We still have much to do.

<74>   Yet Congress has voted to cut environmental enforce-
ment by 25 percent. That means more toxic chemicals in our
water, more smog in our air, more pesticides in our food.

<75>   Lobbyists for {the} polluters have been allowed to write
their own loopholes into bills to weaken laws that protect the
health and safety of our children. {And some in this Congress
want to make} [Some say that the] taxpayers [should] pick up
the tab for toxic waste and let polluters (who can afford to fix
it) off the hook.

<76>   I challenge Congress {to reverse those priorities} [to
reexamine those policies, and to reverse them]. *APPLAUSE*
{I say the polluters should pay.} (This issue has not been a
partisan issue. The most significant environmental gains in
the last 30 years were made under a Democratic Congress
and President Richard Nixon. We can work together. We
have to believe some basic things.) (Do you believe) We can
expand the economy without hurting the environment. (I do.)
{In fact} (Do you believe) we can create more jobs over the
long run by cleaning {it} [the environment] up. (I know we
can. That should be our commitment.) *APPLAUSE*

<77>   We must challenge businesses and communities to take
more initiative in protecting the environment and (we have
to) make it easier for them to do {so} [it]. To businesses, {we
are} [this administration is] saying: If you can find a cheaper,
more efficient way than government regulations require to
meet tough pollution standards, {then} do it—as long as you
do it right.

<78>   To communities, we say: We must strengthen commu-
nity right-to-know laws requiring polluters to disclose their
emissions, but you {must} [have to] use the information to
work with business to cut pollution. People do have a right
to know that their air and water are safe. *APPLAUSE*

<79>   Our sixth challenge is to maintain America's leadership
in the fight for freedom and peace (throughout the world).

<80> Because of American leadership, more people than ever before live free and at peace, and Americans have known 50 years of prosperity and security. We owe thanks especially to our veterans of World War II. *APPLAUSE* (I would like to say) To Senator Bob Dole, and all {the others in this chamber and throughout our country who fought in World War II and all the conflicts} [others in this chamber who fought in World War II, and to all others on both sides of the aisle who have fought bravely in all our conflicts] since, I salute your service (and so does the American people). *APPLAUSE*

<81> All over the world, (even after the Cold War,) people still look to us. And trust us to help them seek the blessings of peace and freedom.

<82> But as the Cold War fades, voices of isolation say America should retreat from its responsibilities. I say they are wrong. The threats we Americans face respect no nation's borders. (Think of them:) terrorism, the spread of weapons of mass destruction, organized crime, drug trafficking, ethnic and religious hatred, aggression by rogue states, environmental degradation. If we fail to address these threats today, we will suffer the consequences {of our neglect tomorrow} [in all our tomorrows]. *APPLAUSE*

<83> (Of course) We can't be everywhere. (Of course) We can't do everything. But where our interests and our values are at stake—and where we can make a difference—America must lead.

<84> We must not be isolationist. {or} [We must not be] the world's policeman. But we can (and should) be the world's (very) best peacemaker. By keeping our military strong, by using diplomacy where we can, and force where we must, by working with others to share the risk and the cost of our efforts, America is making a difference for people here and around the world.

<85> For the first time since the dawn of the nuclear age, (for the first time since the dawn of the nuclear age,) there {are no} [is not a single] Russian missile{s} pointed at America's children. *APPLAUSE* North Korea has now frozen its dangerous nuclear weapons program. In Haiti, the dictators are

gone, democracy has a new day, {and} the flow of desperate refugees to our shores has subsided.

<86>   Through tougher trade deals for America, over 80 of them, we have opened markets abroad, and now exports are at an all-time high, growing faster than imports and creating (good) American jobs. *APPLAUSE*

<87>   We stood with those taking risks for peace, in Northern Ireland, where Catholic and Protestant children now tell their parents that violence must never return, {and} in the Middle East, where Arabs and Jews, who once seemed destined to fight forever, now share knowledge, (and) resources and (even) dreams.

<88>   And, we stood up for peace in Bosnia. Remember the skeletal prisoners, the mass graves, the campaigns of rape and torture, (the) endless lines of refugees, the threat of a spreading war, all these (threats, all these) horrors have now {given} [begun to give] way to the hope of peace. Now our troops and a strong NATO, together with {its} [our] new partners from Central Europe and elsewhere, are helping that peace to take hold.

<89>   (As all of you know, I was just there with a bipartisan Congressional group, and I was so proud not only of what our troops were doing, but in the pride they evidenced in what they were doing. They knew what America's mission in this world is, and they were proud to be carrying it out.) *APPLAUSE*

<90>   Through these efforts, we have enhanced the security of the American people. But (make no mistake about it,) important challenges remain. The Start II Treaty with Russia will cut our nuclear stockpiles by another 25 percent; I urge the Senate to ratify it—now. *APPLAUSE*

<91>   We must end the race to create new nuclear weapons by signing a truly comprehensive nuclear test ban treaty—this year. (As we remember what happened in the Japanese subway,) We can outlaw poison gas forever, if the Senate ratifies the Chemical Weapons Convention—this year. *APPLAUSE* We can intensify the fight against terrorists and organized criminals at home and abroad if Congress passes

the antiterrorism legislation I proposed after the Oklahoma City bombing—now. *APPLAUSE*

<92> We can help more people move from hatred to hope (all across the world, in our own interest), if Congress gives us the means to remain the world's leader for peace. *APPLAUSE*

<93> (My fellow Americans,) The six challenges I have discussed thus far are for all {Americans} [of us]. But our seventh challenge is (really) America's challenge {to us here} [for those of us in this hallowed hall] tonight: to reinvent our government and make our democracy work for them.

<94> Last year, this Congress applied to itself the laws {that} it applies to everyone else. *APPLAUSE* (This Congress) banned gifts and meals from lobbyists. {It} [This Congress] forced lobbyists to disclose who pays them and what legislation they are trying to pass or kill. (This Congress did that.) I applaud you for {that} [it]. *APPLAUSE*

<95> Now I challenge Congress to go further: (to) curb special interest influence in politics by passing the first truly bipartisan campaign finance reform bill in a generation. *APPLAUSE*

<96> (You Republicans and Democrats alike can) Show the American people we can limit spending and that we can open the airwaves to all candidates. *APPLAUSE*

<97> {And} I (also) appeal to Congress to pass the line item veto you promised the American people. *APPLAUSE*

<98> {We are} [Our administration is] working hard to create a government that works better and costs less. Thanks to the work of Vice-President Gore, we are eliminating 16,000 pages of unnecessary rules and regulations, {and} shifting more decision making out of Washington back to states and local communities.

<99> As we move into {an} [the] era of balanced budgets and smaller government, we must work in new ways to enable people to make the most of their own lives.

<100> We are helping America's communities, not with (more) bureaucracy, but with (more) {opportunity} [opportunities]. Through our successful empowerment zones and community development banks, we are helping people find jobs, {and} [to] start businesses. And with tax incentives for companies

that clean up abandoned industrial property, {bringing} [we can bring] jobs back to {the} places that desperately (desperately) need them.

<101>   But there are some areas that the federal government (should not leave, and) {must} [should] address {directly} and (address) strongly. One of these (areas) is the problem of illegal immigration. After years {and years} of neglect, this administration has taken a strong stand to stiffen protection {on} [of] our borders.

<102>   We are increasing border controls by 50 percent; we are increasing inspections to prevent the hiring of illegal immigrants. And tonight, I announce I will sign an executive order to deny federal contracts to businesses that hire illegal immigrants. *APPLAUSE*

<103>   Let me be (very) clear (about this): we are still a nation of immigrants; (we should be proud of it.) {we honor all those immigrants who are working hard to become new citizens} [We should honor every legal immigrant here working hard to be a good citizen, working hard to become a new citizen]. But we are also a nation of laws.

<104>   I want to say a special word (now) to those who work for our federal government. Today, the federal workforce is 200,000 employees smaller than (it was) the day I took office (as President) *APPLAUSE* {The} [Our] federal government is the smallest it has been in 30 years, and it is getting smaller every day. Most of {my} [our] fellow Americans probably {didn't} [don't] know that, and there's a good reason (a good reason). The remaining federal workforce is composed of (hardworking) Americans who are (now) working harder and working smarter (than ever before) to make sure that the quality of our services does not decline. *APPLAUSE*

<105>   (I'd like to give you one example) {Take} [His name is] Richard Dean. He is a 49-year-old Vietnam veteran who has worked for Social Security for 22 years (now). Last year, he was hard at work in the federal building in Oklahoma City when the {terrorist} blast killed 169 people and brought the rubble down (all) around him.

<106>   He re-entered the building four times {and} [he] saved lives of three women. He is here with us this evening. I want

to recognize Richard and applaud both his public service and his extraordinary (personal) heroism. *APPLAUSE*

<107>   But {Richard's} [Richard Dean's] story doesn't end there. This last November, he was forced out of his office when the government shut down.

<108>   And the second time the government shut down, he continued helping Social Security recipients, but he was working without pay.

<109>   On behalf of Richard Dean and his family (and all the other people who are out there, working everyday, doing a good job for the American people), I challenge all of you in this chamber: never—ever—shut the federal government down again. *APPLAUSE*

<110>   And on behalf of all Americans, especially those who need their Social Security payments at the beginning of March, I (also) challenge (the) Congress to preserve the full faith and credit of the United States, to honor the obligations of this great nation as we have for 220 years, to rise above partisanship and pass a straightforward extension of the debt limit. {Show them} [And show the people] that America keeps its word. *APPLAUSE*

<111>   (I know that this evening) I have asked a lot {of America this evening} [of Congress and even more from America]. But I am confident. When Americans work together in their homes, their schools, their churches (and synagogues), their civic groups, {or at work} [their workplace], they can meet any challenge.

<112>   I say again: the era of big government is over. But we can't go back to the era of fending for yourself. We {must} [have to] go forward, to the era of working together—as a community, as a team, as one America—with all of us reaching across {the} [these] lines that divide us, {rejecting} [the] division, (the) discrimination {and} [the] rancor, (we have to reach across it)to find common ground. We {must} [have got to] work together (if we want America to work). *APPLAUSE*

<113>   I want you to meet two (more) people tonight who do (just) that. Lucius Wright is a teacher in the Jackson, Mississippi, public school system, a Vietnam veteran. He has

created groups that help inner-city children turn away from gangs and build futures they can believe in.

<114> Sergeant Jennifer Rodgers is a police officer in Oklahoma City. Like Richard Dean, she helped (to) pull her fellow citizens out of the rubble and deal with that awful tragedy. She reminds us that, in their response to that atrocity, the people of Oklahoma City lifted {us all} [all of us] with their basic sense of decency and community.

<115> Lucius Wright and Jennifer Rogers are special Americans. (And) I have the honor to announce tonight that they are the very first of several thousand Americans who will be chosen to carry the Olympic torch on its long journey from Los Angeles to the centennial of the modern Olympics in Atlanta this summer not because they are star athletes, but because they are star citizens—community heroes meeting America's challenges—(they are) our real champions.
APPLAUSE

<116> Now each of us must hold high the torch of citizenship in our own lives. But none of us can finish the race alone. We can only achieve our destiny together, one hand, one generation, one American connecting to another.

<117> There have always been things we could do together, dreams we could make real—which we could never have done on our own. We Americans have forged our identity, our very union, from {every} [the very] point of view {and} [that we can accommodate] every point on the planet, (every different opinion). But we {are} [must be] bound {together} by a faith more powerful than any doctrine{s} that divide[s] us—by our belief in progress, our love of liberty and our relentless search for common ground. America has always sought and always risen to {the} [every] challenge.

<118> Who would say that, having come so far together, we will not go forward from here? Who would say that this Age of Possibility is not for all Americans?

<119> {America} [Our country] is—and always has been—a great and good {country} [nation]. But the best is yet to come. If we all do our part. Thank you. God bless you, and God bless the *United* States of America.

Review of the Address

Ethos

Remember that a persuasive *ethos* demonstrates practical wisdom, moral virtue, and goodwill. Clinton's attempt to establish such an *ethos* early in the speech is clear. In paragraphs 4–6, he offers a set of statistics on unemployment, inflation, and job creation as well as a general assessment of the crime, poverty, and teen pregnancy rates. By doing this, he surveys very concisely a wide range of social and economic categories, demonstrates that he is aware of their importance and is monitoring their status, and tells the public that he has their best interests in mind. "I am a president," he suggests, "who both knows about and cares about the quality of life in the United States."

The president reinforces his practical wisdom by stressing the practical and the possible throughout the speech. The title published with the predelivery version of the speech is "The Age of Possibility," a concept Clinton stresses by demonstrating his own general sense of the historical development of the United States, from an agricultural age in the nineteenth century to an industrial age in the twentieth century to the current technological age <7>. Clinton's practical wisdom, or *phronesis,* is evident in the organization of the speech into six topics:

The family   <22–35>

Education   <36–43>

Economic security for workers   <44–57>

Crime   <58–70>

The environment   <71–78>

World peace   <79–92>)

Clinton's discussion of these six topics indicates that he is a man with wide-ranging awareness. He attempts to reinforce that impression by offering a series of specific proposals, or challenges, related to each area: for instance, the requirement of a "V" chip in TV sets; a tuition tax deduction for college students and their parents; support for a law expanding health coverage; funding for 100,000 new police; and the denial of federal contracts to companies hiring illegal immigrants.

In sum, what we observe in the course of the speech is *phronesis*— that is, practical wisdom or common sense—demonstrated through facility at the levels of both the general and the specific. Clinton means to show that he is a president who grasps both the big picture and the practical details.

Clinton's *arete,* or moral virtue, is demonstrated through his repeated emphasis on the quality of life of ordinary citizens and his repeated belief in fundamental values <6>. His concern for both values and the quality of life is most focused in paragraph 40, in which Clinton calls for school uniforms in connection with both "character education" and the reduction in gang violence.

Remember that this president is one whose own moral virtue has been under attack. As a candidate, he was accused of marital infidelity, and as president, he has been named in a sexual harassment suit. Further, both Bill Clinton and Hillary Rodham Clinton have been associated with an illegal investment scheme, known as Whitewater. In the face of such challenges to Clinton's own *ethos,* he adds a paragraph noting his love for and devotion to the First Lady <23> in a tribute that praises her moral virtue and implies that she—because she is a wonderful wife and magnificent mother and dedicated to improving the lives of families—could not be involved in anything illegal. At the same time, he represents his own fidelity to her and to the integrity of the family. The telecast of the speech featured the president gazing intently and warmly at the First Lady (who sat with their daughter, Chelsea), while his tribute to Mrs. Clinton drew a long round of applause from those in the chamber.

Eunoia, or goodwill, is largely expressed in statements of appreciation for others and confidence in good outcomes. Often, a political speaker will try to show that his or her goodwill is greater than that of the opponent. For Bill Clinton to do so in this speech, he must propose that he cares more about the American people than the Republicans do. He stresses his greater goodwill most directly in paragraphs 74–76, when he attacks Republican cuts in environmental safeguards and then calls on Congress to reverse direction. The president's greater goodwill is also stressed at several points in the speech that mention the hardships that federal workers suffered when their pay was frozen. He issues a warning to the Republican legislators who (according to some accounts of the situation) allowed this to happen: "Never—ever—shut the federal government down again" <109>.

While Clinton seeks to establish his greater goodwill on behalf of the American people, he also stresses again and again an attitude of goodwill toward Congress itself—in particular, his confidence in bipartisan cooperation. Some commentators have called this speech "conciliatory," to the extent that the president repeatedly mentions his willingness to work together with the Republican leadership and stresses words such as *united, together,* and *bipartisan.* This conciliatory tone is especially evident in the sentences that were added to paragraph 19, in which the president stresses all that he has learned from both Republicans and Democrats and the importance of resolving their differences.

Pathos

Pathos refers to the arousal of emotions or a state of mind that has an emotional component. Typically, the State of the Union address tries to arouse good feelings about the president and his programs, largely through evoking one of the states of mind that Aristotle describes in his discussion of *pathos:* the *confidence* of the audience. To this purpose, Clinton initially emphasizes the state of the union as strong and healthy <4>. Note that at this point, Clinton receives his first major round of applause, which indicates a positive emotional response from the audience. Strong applause also accompanies his declaration that "the era of big government is over" <11>. This statement is one of Clinton's appeals to another state of mind that Aristotle discusses: *friendliness.* One way to evoke friendliness in an audience is to identify a common enemy; for conservative voters and politicians, who typically want less government regulation and lower taxes, big government has been a declared enemy for some time. Here, Clinton makes it his enemy, too.

A word about applause: While applause typically indicates the success of a pathetic appeal and should prompt us to ask what states of mind and emotions are being evoked, applause in the context of the State of the Union address serves other functions, as well. Some applause is merely ceremonial: The president receives a long standing ovation when his entrance into the chamber is announced and another when he is introduced by the speaker of the house. At other times, the applause is partisan: The Democrats applaud certain policies and programs that the Republicans do not. At a number of moments during the speech, Vice-President Gore can be seen standing and applauding behind the president, while House Speaker Gingrich sits nonresponsive. The Republican side is notably reserved when Clinton calls upon Congress to re-examine its policies on the environment, suggesting that the Republican Congress has gone easy on polluters <74–76>. It is interesting to observe that throughout the speech, Democratic and Republican leaders—such as the vice-president, the speaker of the house, and senior members of Congress seated in the chamber—cue their party members about when to applaud, when to rise, and when to remain silent. In many cases, then, we are not observing the sort of applause that greeted Dudley Field Malone's speech on the importance of truth. That was a spontaneous emotional response, clearly indicating the persuasive force of Malone's speech, while the applause greeting the president is often staged and even predictable.

The quotation at the beginning of this chapter from Carmen Rios represents a common emotion that modern politicians seek to address: *hopelessness*. The perception that government is ineffective in making substantial improvements in people's lives (whether true or not) is widespread in the United States, leading to the sort of apathy we see in Rios, who has decided not to watch the speech. For those citizens who are watching the speech, the president wants to replace hopelessness and cynicism with confidence and optimism as well as approval.

Most of the president's proposals speak to a middle-class, middle-aged, conservative constituency—people who worry about having enough money to send their children to college, about crime and gangs invading their neighborhoods, about the erosion of moral values in the entertainment industry, and about rising taxes that, to their minds, pay for bloated social programs. Clinton offers specific proposals in all these areas, several of them tied to specific dollar amounts that citizens would receive (for instance, a $10,000 tax deduction for college tuition <43>), as a way of countering attitudes like that expressed by Carmen Rios. Clinton also offers proposals of direct benefit to lower-income or un-employed workers (for instance, a $2,600 voucher for job training and a higher minimum wage <47–48>). Such proposals are tied directly to what the president hopes is a universal value for his audience: hard work. The word *work* appears in the speech 36 times, most often in connection with people's efforts to get and hold jobs; clearly, the president is appealing to the work ethic that has been generally identified with American moral virtue throughout this country's history. Of course, the proposal to raise the minimum wage also appeals to the compassion that Congress and the public feel toward those people who are suffering because of low wages.

Logos

We have already defined *logos* with reference to enthymemes, maxims, examples, and certain stylistic features that have a psychological appeal, such as metaphor and anaphora. All of these elements of persuasion are present in the State of the Union address. As noted in Chapter 1, an enthymeme often follows a *causal* structure, with phrases such as *if this, then that* or with causal signposts such as *because, for, since,* and *when.*

Enthymemes abound in the president's address, and many of them have an explicit if/then structure. Each of the enthymemes in the excerpts that follow leaves out a basic premise that makes its reasoning more complete; the audience is expected to supply that premise. Following each enthymeme, a possible left-out premise is stated in brackets:

If we have stronger families, we will have a stronger America. <22>
[Strong families contribute to the strength of a country.]

If your family has separated, you must pay your child support. <35>
[Supporting one's children is a basic parental obligation.]

If our working families are going to succeed in the new economy, they must be able to buy health insurance policies that they don't lose when they change jobs or when someone in the family gets sick. <53>
[Healthy workers are more successful workers.]

America cannot become stronger, if they [those who need Medicare and Medicaid] become weaker. <54>
[A strong nation requires a physically strong population.]

If we fail to address these threats [of worldwide crime and terrorism] today, we will suffer the consequences in all our tomorrows. <82>
[A global problem unaddressed affects the future of us all.]

We have got to work together if we want America to work. <112>
[A well-functioning nation requires unity and cooperation from its citizens and legislators.]

To the extent that the audience is supplying premises consistent with President Clinton's enthymemes, they are persuading themselves that the enthymemes are valid. The audience must supply even more missing material when faced with a maxim, that is, a single proposition. Some of the maxims that Clinton offers are:

> America was built on challenges, not promises. <21>
>
> Every diploma ought to mean something. <38>
>
> People do have a right to know that their air and water are safe. <78>

A metaphor, like an enthymeme or maxim, also requires psychological work on the part of the audience. The audience is asked to visualize or understand one thing in terms of another. President George Bush relied heavily on metaphor in his 1989 inaugural address in sentences such as the following:

> But this is a time when the future seems a door you can walk right through, into a room called tomorrow.

The metaphor here is explicitly stated: "The future is an open door." If the audience understands that both the future and the open door share common elements, they will grasp the association and, in this case, be moved to share the general attitude Bush is advancing: optimism about the future.

One of the central metaphorical moments in Clinton's speech also advances optimism:

> Now each of us must hold high the torch of citizenship in our own lives. But none of us can finish the race alone. We can only achieve our destiny together, one hand, one generation, one American connecting to another. <116>

The two main metaphors at work here are "Citizenship is a torch" and "Life is a [communal] race." Both seek to stress central themes of the speech as a whole: burning pride in one's citizenship and responsibilities and cooperation with others.

Speech Acts

The quotation from John Forst given at the beginning of this chapter highlights the ways in which an audience's perception of a speaker's motives can affect their evaluation of the speech. Such perceptions are often predetermined and are connected to the *ethos* of the speaker. For instance, in order to maintain the positive *ethos* of their own party, Republican respondents to Clinton's speech often denied that it was an act of practical wisdom and goodwill; rather, they claimed, this speech was simply an act of electioneering. Echoing citizen John Forst, Republican Representative Henry Hyde of Illinois called the speech "a State of the Campaign speech, not a State of the Union."

Such evaluations call into question what speech act theorists would call the *performative force* of the president's address. The president is not *reporting* on the State of the Union, Forst suggests; he is *campaigning* for re-election. There are always numerous opinions about the performative force of a State of the Union address. In this case, they included the opinions by some commentators that the speech was "conciliatory" and by others that the speech was—as Senator Bob Dole put it—a "contradiction" because the president's words did not match his actions while in office.

Significantly, Clinton frames the whole speech as an explicit performative, namely, as a series of challenges. The word *challenge* or *challenges* appears 50 times. Clinton speaks of an improved future as a challenge all Americans should face together, and he issues specific challenges to the following:

Broadcast industry   <26>

Cigarette manufacturers   <28>

Congress   <30, 43, 47, 48, 51, 61, 63, 68, 76, 95, 110>

Welfare recipients   <31>

Employers and businesses   <31, 51, 77>

American families, and in particular, divorced fathers   <34–35>

Educators   <38–40>

Parents   <41>

Housing authorities   <65>

State governments   <66>

A challenge is a kind of dare, and as with any dare, not answering it is conventionally believed to be a sign of weakness. The State of the Union speech might be characterized as an extended dare, aimed especially at Congress and, in this sense, is an astute strategy on Clinton's part. Here is a Democratic president facing a Republican majority, a president who is, from certain political perspectives, in a position of weakness. To dare his audience is to project weakness onto them and thus divert that identity from himself. If the audience takes up the dare, they will be acting in accordance with the president's proposals and policies; if they refuse the dare, they will be admitting weakness. By choosing the *challenge/dare* as the explicit performative in this address, then, Clinton is trying to ensure that he will win the advantage, one way or another. The choice of *challenge* as the explicit performative in this speech counterbalances other elements we have noted earlier as *conciliatory*. By framing this speech as a series of challenges, the president can, in effect, taunt Congress at the same time that he pledges cooperation with them.

Dramatism

The relationship of President Clinton to his audience constitutes a kind of drama that can be illuminated with reference to Kenneth Burke's dramatism and specifically with reference to the terms of his pentad: Act, Scene, Agent, Agency, and Purpose. As noted in Chapter 1, concerning the O. J. Simpson criminal trial, how we name any one of these categories will affect how we name all the rest and will influence our understanding and evaluation of the drama we are investigating. If, for instance, the Act that President Clinton is performing is called a *challenge,* labels for the other terms might be as follow:

       Act: Challenge

   Scene: Democratic president facing Republican Congress

   Agent: Bill Clinton

 Agency: State of the Union address

Purpose: Gaining advantage over the audience

The label we give the speech indicates how we are persuaded to regard it, and that depends upon the drama that we have constructed. Senator Bob Dole, who became Clinton's Republican opponent in the 1996 election, characterized the speech as a *defense* rather than a *challenge,* thus choosing a performative term that put Clinton in a position of weakness. Referring to Clinton's recent veto of a Republican budget bill, a veto that Clinton mentioned in paragraph 49, Dole said, "The president has chosen to defend, with his veto, a welfare system that no one can defend, for it is a daily assault on the values of self-reliance and family." Referring to Clinton's proposal for a networked computer system in U.S. schools, Dole said, "He has chosen to defend an education establishment whose goal is to operate every school in America by remote control from Washington." With such remarks, Dole suggested the following pentad:

> **Act:** Defense of the welfare system and educational establishment
>
> **Scene:** State of the Union address
>
> **Agent:** "Big Brother" (a label given by Dole to Clinton, referring to the totalitarian state in George Orwell's *1984*)
>
> **Agency:** Big government
>
> **Purpose:** Corruption of American values and federal control of education

When John Forst and Henry Hyde both called Clinton's address a campaign speech (and Hyde further noted Clinton's unfair criticism of Republicans), they suggested the following pentad:

> **Act:** Campaign speech
>
> **Scene:** 1996 presidential election
>
> **Agent:** Democratic candidate for president
>
> **Agency:** State of the Union address
>
> **Purpose:** Showing up Republicans

When Carmen Rios chose not to watch the speech, saying, "I feel there is nothing that can be done about anything," she was implicitly naming the Scene in terms of her own mood, one of hopelessness and cynicism. Her remark suggested the following pentad:

Act:	State of the Union address
Scene:	Hopelessness and cynicism
Agent:	President Clinton
Agency:	Ineffectual government
Purpose:	False hope

Negotiating Identification

It is worth noting that the word *we* appears over 100 times in the course of Clinton's speech, and the word *our* appears over 140 times. This is not remarkable for a political speech but does point to *identification* as a primary motive; these words indicate Clinton's attempt to identify himself as part of a larger group or population. The word *you*, on the other hand, is used less frequently, 33 times, and in a number of those cases, it indicates a group from which the president wants to detach himself:

To the media: I say you should create movies, and CDs and television shows you would want your own children and grandchildren to enjoy.   <25>

Market your products [cigarettes] to adults, if you wish—but draw the line on children.   <28>

But let's all admit something about that [payment of child support] too: A check will never substitute for a parent's love and guidance, and only you can make the decision to help raise your children—no matter who you are, how low or high your station in life, it is the most basic human duty of every American to do that job to the best of his or her ability.   <35>

I challenge you to raise their minimum wage.   <48>

From now on, the rule for residents who commit crimes and peddle drugs should be: one strike and you're out.   <65>

To businesses, we are saying: If you can find a cheaper, more efficient way than government regulations require to meet tough pollution standards, do it—as long as you do it right. <77>

I challenge all of you in this chamber: never—ever—shut the federal government down again. <109>

In general, we can say that *negotiating identification* is a central element in any political speech. By surveying a broad range of topics in his demonstration of *phronesis,* President Clinton also stresses his identification with a broad spectrum of the American public. At the same time, he is giving his speech great scope and circumference and allowing for what Kenneth Burke would call a *margin of overlap* with a number of different kinds of people with different interests. In order to negotiate identification—that is, in order to indicate the extent of his overlap with the interests of the audience—Clinton will, at times, be quite absolute about where he draws the line. The negotiation of identification is apparent in paragraphs 101–103, where Clinton addresses the problem of illegal immigration. There, he acknowledges that "we are a nation of immigrants" but "we are also a nation of laws," thus indicating that his identification/margin of overlap does not include all immigrants but only lawful immigrants.

President Clinton's negotiation of identification is perhaps most labored in paragraph 19, to which he added several sentences of material when delivering the speech, praising the good ideas that result when Republicans and Democrats work together. Passages like this had some members of the audience, such as Democratic Representative Luis Gutierrez of Chicago, saying that "It sounded like a Republican making the speech." In other words, for Gutierrez, Clinton's identification with the opposition had, at moments, gone too far. Responses such as Gutierrez's indicate the supple nature of identification as it often operates in political speeches, where a speaker must try to be persuasive to a number of persuasions.

Summary

Democratic President Bill Clinton delivered his 1996 State of the Union address while facing substantial challenges to his persuasive abilities: a Republican majority Congress; a cynical and increasingly conservative public; charges against his and his wife's personal integrity; and an election just 10 months away. In the course of his speech, Clinton drew from elements of persuasion we have discussed throughout this book.

In an attempt to establish an effective *ethos*, Clinton emphasized his practical wisdom by displaying a comprehensive awareness of a range of national and international issues and by focusing on certain specific proposals. He demonstrated moral virtues through repeated statements emphasizing fundamental values and by stressing the integrity of his own marriage and family. He exhibited goodwill toward U.S. citizens by arguing that he had been more protective of their welfare than had the Republicans in Congress, and he showed goodwill toward Congress by pledging to cooperate with them in a bipartisan spirit.

In its appeals to *pathos*, the State of the Union address generally tried to arouse confidence in the president and his administration. To this end, the speech was deliberately designed and delivered in order to evoke many instances of applause, which may tend to illustrate confidence in the president to a viewing audience. Aware that a growing number of citizens were cynical about the government's ability to improve the quality of life, Clinton voiced proposals calculated to improve opportunities for better jobs and wages. With such proposals, he attempted both to cultivate more optimistic citizens and to emphasize both compassion and hard work as virtues that he wanted the audience to share.

The *logos* of the speech made frequent use of enthymemes, maxims, and metaphors, all of which require the audience to supply missing premises and associations. To the extent that a speech requires psychological work on the part of the audience, it involves them actively in the process of persuasion.

How audience members labeled Clinton's address as a speech act often depended on their political affiliations: Some Republicans claimed that the president was campaigning rather than reporting on the State of the Union. Clinton himself characterized the speech as a series of challenges; putting himself in the position of challenger adds strength to his *ethos* and puts his opponents on the defensive.

When Senator Bob Dole characterized Clinton's speech as a defense rather than a challenge, he not only changed the identity of the address as a speech act but also altered the dramatistic relations among the Act, Scene, Agent, Agency, and Purpose. It is possible to construct a number of different Burkean pentads to indicate how different observers would define the drama of the presentation. We might suggest that one primary purpose for the speech was *identification.* Clinton tried to voice concepts and values with which his audience would identify and also stressed identification through the frequent use of the pronouns *we* and *our.*

❖ Questions to Ask Yourself

One of the oldest questions debated by rhetoricians and philosophers has to do with the relationship between *eloquence* and *virtue.* Some have argued that a person who is morally virtuous will be more likely to be eloquent, that is, more likely to speak or write effectively and persuasively. Others have argued that through training in eloquence, speakers and writers become more virtuous; their heightened awareness of the complex relationship among speaker, audience, and subject matter makes them more sensitive and receptive to different points of view. Still others have argued that eloquence leads to vice, rather than virtue, proposing that an eloquent speaker often uses that talent to fool people. And some have maintained that eloquence and virtue are unrelated.

Where does this chapter—and this book, in general—leave us in deciding on the relationship between eloquence and virtue? Does greater awareness of the elements of persuasion and the ability to employ them make one a better person in some respect? Does any evidence in this chapter or this book suggest that there is some relationship between eloquence and virtue? Explain your answers.

❖ Writing Exercise

Check your college library for collections of current political speeches. One publication you might search for is *Vital Speeches of the Day,* which is published twice a month and includes a variety of public speeches by political, business, and academic leaders. Often, the transcripts of such speeches will identify the audience to which they were addressed.

Focus on one speech or one section of a speech, and locate elements of *ethos, pathos,* and *logos* that contribute to its persuasive effect. Write a brief essay in which you discuss the ways in which these elements work together.

❖ *Persuasive Strategies for Student Writers*

Read your writing aloud several times while you are composing it, as if it is to be delivered as a speech. Reading aloud can help you pick up simple errors, unintended stressings, and missing information. Moreoever, doing so can help give you some indication of how your writing will sound to readers as they read.

Glossary

Note: Bold words within definitions appear as entries elsewhere in this Glossary.

anaphora   The repetition of a word or phrase in successive statements, which can serve to reinforce a main theme or help emotionally involve an audience. One famous instance of anaphora is Martin Luther King, Jr.'s, repetition of "I have a dream" in the speech he delivered during the March on Washington on August 28, 1963 (see pp. 47–49).

Aristotle (384–322 BCE)   A Greek philosopher whose work *Rhetoric*, written between 360 and 334 BCE, has influenced many subsequent theories of persuasion. This work is best known for developing a psychology of audience (see pp. 4–5).

Austin, J. L. (1911–1960)   A language philosopher who developed **speech act theory**, which examines how language works in social exchanges. In 1955, he delivered a series of lectures on this subject, which were published after his death in 1962 under the title *How to Do Things with Words* (see pp. 12–13).

Burke, Kenneth (1897–1993)   A critic and theorist who understands persuasion as a process of **identification**. He allows us to think of any persuasion situation **dramatistically** as an interaction among an Act, Scene, Agent, Agency, and Purpose (see pp. 18–20).

circumference   As used by Kenneth **Burke**, this term refers to the inclusiveness of a definition or concept. Defining *knowledge* as "information taught in school" creates a smaller circumference than defining it as "the body of facts, concepts, and skills gained through a variety of experiences." Circumference is the counterpart to **scope** (see pp. 53–55).

dramatism A theory of the relationship between language and human relations, developed by Kenneth **Burke.** In order to understand fully what any statement can mean, we must understand it as an Act produced in a Scene by an Agent using a certain means (Agency) for a Purpose. Working through this pentad of Act, Scene, Agent, Agency, and Purpose helps us understand the drama of communication and persuasion (see pp. 18–20).

enthymeme A claim that invites the audience to supply missing premises. "To get an education, students must have access to the Internet" is a claim that requires the premise "Material on the Internet is educational." For an audience that holds this premise, the enthymeme is persuasive. **Aristotle** makes the enthymeme central to persuasion (see pp. 10–11).

ethos The character of a speaker or writer engaged in persuasion. **Aristotle** associates *ethos* with practical wisdom, moral virtue, and goodwill toward the audience and advises speakers to exhibit these characteristics through the content of their speeches (see pp. 7–8).

identification As used by Kenneth **Burke,** the process of discovering common interests with another individual or group. Identification may mean finding shared goals, experiences, beliefs, or abilities (see p. 79).

ideology As used by Kenneth **Burke,** an "aggregate of beliefs" that includes "what the [audience] considers desirable." Our ideology determines how we interpret and respond to what we read and hear. With this definition of *ideology,* Burke brings it close to **Aristotle's** *pathos* (see p. 5).

illocutionary act A statement that performs a specific action. "I promise to be on time" performs the act of promising. J. L. **Austin** introduces illocution in his **speech act theory** as a kind of **performative** (see pp. 16–17).

kairos Timeliness. This concept stresses the importance of saying the right thing at the right time. In persuasion, *kairos* operates when a speaker or writer times a statement to coincide with the audience's readiness to understand and accept it (see pp. 105–06).

logos   The logical reasoning expressed in speech or writing. For **Aristotle,** the **enthymeme** is central to *logos* (see pp. 10–12).

metaphor   Creation of an unconventional meaning by associating words in two unlike categories: for example, "School is a circus" (see p. 62).

pathos   The emotions or state of mind of an audience. According to **Aristotle,** the emotional response of any audience to a speaker or writer will depend on the audience's beliefs, values, desires, and expectations (see pp. 8–10).

performative   An utterance that performs some action, such as promising, warning, or commanding. An explicit performative names the action, as in "I'm warning you; don't play with fire." An implicit performative leaves the action unstated, as in "Don't play with fire." Performatives are discussed as part of J. L. **Austin's speech act theory** (see pp. 13–17).

perlocutionary act   An audience's interpretation of a **performative.** The perlocutionary force of an utterance can vary, according to the circumstances in which it is delivered: "There's one more piece of pizza" might be understood as *offering* the pizza, *warning* against eating the last piece, *informing* about how much is left, *regretting* that all of it wasn't eaten, or *complaining* that too much has been eaten. J. L. **Austin** introduces perlocution in his **speech act theory** (see p. 16).

scope   The context that one consults when defining a concept or issue. For example, people who think about social justice only with reference to the needs and problems of white, middle-class Americans are exercising much less scope than people who consider social justice with reference to individuals from a range of socioeconomic, racial, and ethnic groups. Scope is the counterpart to Kenneth **Burke's circumference** (see pp. 53–55).

speech act theory   Developed by J. L. **Austin,** this theory proposes that we should think about linguistic utterances as **performatives** and ask questions about what sorts of acts particular utterances are performing (see pp. 12–17).

syllogism   A logical statement in which the premises lead to a certain conclusion (see pp. 1–2):

> All advertisements use persuasion.
>
> Television commercials are advertisements.
>
> Television commercials use persuasion.

Index